For the

A Simple Rule of Life

Andy Johnson

Joseph and Daniel

For your journey...

Acknowledgements

A few words of thanks to the people who have helped make this project possible. Paul Salter and Chris Surgenor have given advice and offered editorial help throughout. Thanks for the input and the coffee!

To the other original Rule of Life group members, Danny Rodgers, Reza Pirnia, Will Wrigley, David Humphrey, Paolo Cavallo and Abi Rotimi: thank you for your honesty and willingness to be guinea pigs in this process. Thank you also to Alan and Marilla Logan for giving this material a 'test run' in your home group.

I'm grateful to Revd Peter Mackenzie for creating the environment during my curacy in which I could develop my Rule of Life and begin to share it with others.

Thank you also to Bishop Pete Broadbent, Russell Winfield and Lucy Thompson for your help and kind words of recommendation.

And finally to my wife Andrea whose love and support has made this part of my journey possible. Without you this would not have been a reality and I am grateful to God for you.

Contents

"The idea of a 'Rule of Life' spooks a lot of Christians for whom it's not their language or culture. What Andy Johnson has done is write a guide, in simple language, to working out your own Rule of Life, thoughtfully, prayerfully and gradually. It's a great aid for individuals and for discussion groups – a real challenge to be reflective, to be honest and to be specific in ways that will help you grow as a Christian. Thoroughly recommended."

The Rt Revd Pete Broadbent, Bishop of Willesden

"The richness of For the Journey is underscored by Andy's commitment to living what he has written about. This book was not born in a study but in the realities of everyday life, and has been refined through conversation and application. The result is a book that will help anyone looking for wisdom to help them to journey well with God."

Revd Russell Winfield
Director of Development St Mellitus College, London

"This book offers us an opportunity to consciously and intentionally invite God into every part of our life. Our worth in God's eyes is unquestioned and yet in partnership with Him we can know transformation and increasingly establish a life which honours and glorifies Him. Andy provides us with the challenge and the opportunity to deepen our relationship with God in new and practical ways. It is an easy yet compelling read."

Lucy Thompson, Director, Quest Perspective
www.questperspective.co.uk

Foreword

When Andy Johnson asked me to join the Rule of Life group in September 2015 I really did not know what to expect. Having recently retired from full time employment and with more time available on a personal level, I had already decided that I had a precious opportunity to go deeper into my Christian faith; to explore questions related to my beliefs that I had not the time to think about, let alone resolve. The solution lay of course with the Rule of Life group and the materials that Andy produced for our monthly meetings and which now form the basis of this book.

Meeting every month at Andy's house, the group gathered to discuss and explore the various principles of the Rule of Life that he had drawn up. Our sessions produced some very interesting and challenging discussions and one of the great strengths of Andy's book is that each chapter contains both questions for discussion (ideal for small groups) as well as practical suggestions that can be put into practice. As a group we also enjoyed a monthly visit to a variety of different restaurants in West Ealing living out Andy's view that "There is nothing I love better than sitting around a table with good friends enjoying good food and drink."

As a committed Christian, Andy lives his life in a very sincere way, strongly influenced by the work of the Holy Spirit and the spiritual disciplines he has put in place as part of his everyday routine. In the Rule of Life group he demonstrated his profound commitment to passing on his Christian faith to others.

And in developing the course into a book, Andy has evidenced a strong interest in developing Christian leadership and the role that leadership can play in disseminating the Gospel. His approachable nature, his generosity and his wonderful sense of humour were always evident in the various social functions we enjoyed as a group.

What really makes 'For the Journey' different and such a useful guide for Christians wishing to develop their faith is the practical suggestions that accompany every chapter. These suggestions provide practical strategies for Christian living that have a tangible impact on everyday life and have the potential to be truly transformative in nature. Being part of the Rule of Life group, reading this book and putting into practice some of the suggestions outlined in it has transformed my thinking on the purpose of worship, the Eucharist and the Sabbath. Structured prayer during the day and being able to re-evaluate my relationship with God have deepened my faith and improved my understanding of the God I worship. As Andy would be quick to point out, none of us is the finished article and as part of my journey I intend to read a chapter of this book every month so that I can further reflect on and deepen my faith. I strongly recommend this book to anyone who desires to see transformation in their life and who wishes to walk in a closer relationship with Jesus.

Paul Salter

Introduction

This is a book about choices - the everyday choices that you and I make all day long. I am assuming that you, the reader, have already made one choice - choosing to live your life as a disciple of Jesus: to follow him as best as you are able and to allow that decision to shape your whole life. If I am making too much of an assumption here and you have not in fact made the 'disciple of Jesus' choice then stick with me. You will find this book full of suggestions as to how to live a better life and you might even resolve the 'Jesus' question in the process.

This book is also born out of a frustration with the use of the word 'discipleship'. As a church leader, everywhere I go I see churches finding new and creative ways of saying they are basically going to try and do what Jesus instructed his disciples to do before he returned to his Father.

'Go and make disciples of all nations, baptising them in the name of the Father and of the Son and of the Holy Spirit.' MATTHEW 28:19

There are no surprises here. Jesus said it - we ought to do it and it would be somewhat of a worry if your local church's mission statement indicated a desire to teach its members how to crochet or play poker! So making disciples (of Jesus) is the brief and, unsurprisingly, that is what you find when you trawl through mission statements found on numerous church websites.

So we are pretty much agreed on what we are meant to be doing. This book is more concerned with the how. The trouble with discipleship is it can end up being a somewhat nebulous concept. Am I more of a disciple now than I was this time last year? Am I a better disciple? More to the point, how would I even know? Can you even measure that sort of thing? I'm not sure; which is why you have to trust the process. Do certain things, engage in certain tried and trusted practices and if you do, you know what the end result will look like. A Rule of Life can help you live with intention and purpose in the present moment. It helps you clarify your most important values and then live by them.

For some of you, the word 'Rule' is already ringing alarm bells. Let me see if I can put your mind at rest. The last thing God wants for us, or indeed we need, is any kind of legalism, so confronted with my own frustration around a lack of personal spiritual growth I began work on a framework to follow that would free me to follow Christ in an intentional, meaningful and committed way. The idea of a Rule of Life comes from the Latin word *regula* and suggests a way to regulate or balance one's life in order to stay on an intentional path. Think of it like a trellis that provides support and guidance for a plant as it grows. Using a trellis you can help a plant grow in a certain direction and actively discourage it heading off in another. My Rule of Life is like a trellis for my best intentions and God-given hopes, dreams and ideas. Without structure, growth is sporadic, chaotic and disorderly at best. It wanders where it wants and the end result is not as desired.

My interest in a Rule of Life began when I spent some time studying the life of St. Benedict of Nursia. Born in 480AD in a small town about 100 miles northeast of Rome to noble and wealthy parents, Benedict was sent to Rome to complete his education. This turned out to be a seminal experience as the wild-living and moral laxity that he encountered prompted his decision to change track in search of peace and truth.

Arguably his most significant years were spent leading a monastery at Monte Cassino from about 529AD, where he drew up his famous Rule. Concerned as he was about the complexities of community life, his real passion was to live the Christian life to the fullest and to help those around him do the same. He knew the human heart and its tendency to pull away from the love and protection of God, towards the allure of the world and the sinful nature.

Little has changed today. Many of us deeply desire to grow in love and godliness but end up making little progress, marooned in a malaise of frustration, sin and guilt. It doesn't have to be that way! A simple framework for living: a Rule of Life to help us get it right with God and with each other can go a long way towards growth and maturity in becoming and living as disciples of Jesus.

How easy it is to forget the fact that a person's interior and exterior worlds are so closely connected. The inner world of the spiritual must govern the outer world of activity and so we do well to invest in and nurture that interior / inner world. It was Socrates who said, "May the outward and inward man be one."[1] Spiritual disciplines are the traditional means by which this is done; disciplines like prayer and Bible reading (which is where I am going to begin) facilitate renewal on the inside, which in turn should bring change on the outside as well.

Many of us are quite adept at portraying a 'togetherness' - that all is well in us and within us. But often the reality is something quite different; we are hollow and aching on the inside. Religious noise (our own and that going on all around us) can help mask the reality. But God knows the truth - and so do we if only we were brave enough to stop and face it.

In chapter 1 I'll reference the phenomenon known in Christian circles as the 'Quiet Time'. A time spent each day in prayer and studying the Bible. Typically when enquiring of someone's spiritual health, we might ask "How's your quiet time?" The answer may come in easily measurable terms such as minutes, days, Bible chapters or prayer techniques. The more interesting or telling question to ask might be, "How's your inner / interior life?" Some people don't know they even have one!

---

[1] Socrates prayer from Plato's *Phaedrus*.

In a nutshell, our desire for life should be to get on board with God's plans and purposes for us. To become the people he desires us to be. Ultimately, nothing could be more rewarding than this, nothing more sought after. This is discipleship and I offer this Rule of Life as a means to help make that desire a reality. I offer it as one way (or 12) to embrace, which will help us to cooperate with the Spirit of God who is at work in us. It is my firm belief and testimony that as I began to live this Rule of Life, something began to be formed in me - something good, something spiritual, something of God.

You are free to choose for yourself. Read, understand and learn about my Rule of Life and maybe adopt it for a season and see what God will work out in your life. Alternatively, may this Rule of Life galvanise you to sit down and write your own set of principles to live by. In a sense there is nothing special or magical about my twelve. They may resonate with you and set you on your way to a more fulfilling and God-honouring life. Alternatively they may simply act as a catalyst for you to identify before God the things that are truly important to you so that you can shape your life around them.

'I do not understand what I do.
For what I want to do I do not do, but what I hate I do.'
ROMANS 7:15

Many of us would share this sentiment of the Apostle Paul. We recognise the deficiencies in our own lives and wish we were somehow different. We may or may not 'beat ourselves up' over our failures but at the very least we live with a disappointment concerning them. A Rule of Life can be a gift to us, a helping hand to enable us to become the people we want to be. Not a restricting, limiting set of laws to be followed but actually a means of freedom. The means by which change can come in our lives; how frustration can give way to personal growth and contentment.

Prayerfully consider this Rule of Life, and may it, or a version of it, free you to be the person that you and, more importantly, God wants you to be.

1. Daily Office

**I will make it a priority to pray,
worship and read the Bible every day
and will allow this 'Daily Office' to shape me
and change me from within.**

One day Peter and John were going up to the temple at
the time of prayer - at three in the afternoon.
ACTS 3:1

To clasp the hands in prayer is the beginning of an
uprising against the disorder of the world.
Karl Barth

I came to faith in a church that clearly taught the benefits of a daily time of prayer and Bible reading - we used to call it a 'Quiet Time'. Bible reading notes were widely available to help you make sense of a short passage and spontaneous prayer was meant to take up the rest of the 10-15 minutes. Morning was the very best time to have this 'Quiet Time' after which you were 'good to go' for the rest of the day.

Occasionally I would bump into someone who was honest enough to admit that they found this discipline as hard as I did and not always that fulfilling either. But mostly I laboured on trying my best to keep up with the programme, battling with guilt for failing to pray/read as much as I should.

Growing up in a small market town in Cambridgeshire, my exposure to other faiths was extremely limited and it wasn't until I moved to London in my mid-twenties that I first met people whose pattern of prayer was quite different to my own. As I learned that Muslims (not exclusively) would stop what they were doing to kneel and pray, a chord was struck in my heart. Could I do that, I wondered...?

Fast forward two+ decades and I find myself retreating at Hilfield Friary in Dorset, joining in with the rhythm of the monks of that community. Even though the chapel was cold and uninviting, as I experienced the rhythm of prayer and worship, something was lodged in my heart - a sense that maybe this was what I was looking for. I can't say that a deep spiritual experience took place but rather a sense of my life slowing down and becoming more in step with God's will for me.

Of course, I and quite probably you are not called to live in a monastery so my task since has been to find a way to live as a husband, father and church leader with a God-given routine governing my every day. This year, I may have found it, and it involves four moments....

The first comes at the beginning of the day when I express to God my desire to live this day for Him. I often use Brian Doerksen's 2008 worship song as a simple way to express this:

> Today I choose to follow You
> Today I choose to give my 'yes' to You
> Today I choose to hear Your voice and live
> Today I choose to follow You[2]

I find it helpful to walk through the coming day deliberately calling to mind the tasks, meetings, challenges that lie ahead. Similarly, I bring to mind the people I love and care for and those who I might naturally become anxious about if I weren't entrusting them to God. The other thing I do is work through a cycle of prayer consisting of people or situations about which I intercede.

My second 'moment' comes in the middle of the day; midday is good but find whatever works for you. This acts as a reminder to me to be serious about my already

---

[2] Permission to use granted by Brian & Joyce Doerksen.

stated desire to do the day God's way; to live for him and not be consumed by my own desires and priorities. Believe me, by lunchtime I need that reminder! Setting a phone to chime can remind you it is time to pray.

The Church of England's pattern of prayer provides me with the third opportunity to pray at 5pm each day for Evening Prayer. At my previous church, as clergy we were left to do this on our own until Advent 2014 when as somewhat of a cry for help in a busy season, it was suggested we gather at church for 30 minutes and pray together. Through Advent, these times became such a lifeline that in the New Year we decided to continue the pattern. Often there were just two or three of us but no matter - the encouragement one receives from a regular commitment to pray together is immense. It is thoroughly reviving at the end of a busy day and sustaining ahead of an evening likely to have a meeting of one sort or another scheduled.

This just leaves night prayer, said just before bedtime. This is an opportunity to review the day with God and in so doing express my delight and sadness at how it's gone. Some find St Ignatius' Prayer of Examen[3] helpful to use as a tool to reflect on the day with God; an aid in discerning what God has said and might be saying.

If all of this sounds like a chore or burdensome, then I have miscommunicated. It really is anything but. Rather this pattern of prayer acts as a means by which I can do

---

[3] See www.ignatianspirituality.com/the-examen

what I said to God I wanted to do at the beginning of the day: Today I choose to follow you...

There is nothing special about the suggested times - they can of course be adjusted to suit your own pattern or lifestyle. What I am trying to convey is a mindset worth adopting to help you keep close to God throughout the day.

How utterly ignorant I was in being secretly envious of our Muslim brothers and sisters. I only had to look into the Scriptures to see 'fixed hour prayer' going on before, during and after the time of Christ.

In Psalm 119:164, the Hebrew Psalmist writes "Seven times a day I praise you for your righteous laws." What a lightweight I am in my attempts to snatch four moments every day! Then as the Christian faith itself and the early church was in it's infancy, we see fixed hour prayer being observed or offered:

One day Peter and John were going up to the temple at the time of prayer - at three in the afternoon.
ACTS 3:1

Here, there is clear evidence that this type of prayer was continuing in the early church. There is more evidence later in Acts, when Peter receives his vision from the Lord concerning the all-encompassing nature of the gospel:

About noon.... as they were on their journey...
Peter went up onto the roof to pray.
ACTS 10:9

In the third century, the Desert Fathers, the earliest monastics, adopted this rhythm and saw it as a way of heeding St Paul's exhortation to "pray continually" (1 Thessalonians 5:17). As one group of monks passed the praying 'baton' onto another through the Daily Office, so the on-going cascade of praise and prayer was maintained through the day and across time zones.

For Benedict of Nursia, fixed hour prayer was Opus Dei, the "work of God" and so that remains today. By adopting a rhythm of fixed hour prayer we both do the work of God in interceding for the world and those around us and the work of God is done in us by the Spirit - a transformative work.

Once again, there is nothing magic about the Daily Office except to say that through establishing a rhythm of prayer, worship and Scripture reading in your life, you nourish your soul and give the Holy Spirit room to re-orientate your life back towards God. Midday Prayer[4] (perhaps the hardest one to keep) is particularly helpful in stopping you in your tracks and pointing you back to God in the midst of the busyness. If you find it easy to pray, you are most firmly in the minority. And yet pray we must as it is one of God's most precious gifts to us.

During Holy Communion, in the Eucharistic Prayer, we acknowledge it is our "duty and our joy" to offer God our thanks and praise. This is a helpful way of thinking about

---

[4] Or lunchtime prayer

the Daily Office or fixed hour prayer. Whilst leaving no room for legalism, we are in a sense duty-bound to make time for regular prayer, worship and Scripture reading. And yet it is also our joy as through this we are fed and we become the people we want to be.

When my day is punctuated with regular set times of prayer, I find I am less likely to stray from God's plans and purposes for me and spiral off down an alleyway of "me-ness".

Of course each of us can pray at anytime in any place, with or without the help of form or structure. I just find that despite my best intentions, I don't do that. The bottom line is, this rhythm helps me to pray.

The same could be said for worship and Bible reading. I firmly believe that God is the sole focus of our sung worship and yet it is also my experience that our merciful God reaches out to us as we worship Him. Worshipping Him, does us good! I will explore this more in the next chapter but suffice to say that through listening to a worship song or two at the beginning of the day, I become more ready to pray and read the Scriptures. My heart is settling and my focus re-tuned. Consistently working through the Psalms on a rotation basis can be an aid in this although it is fair to say that some are more worshipful and hope-filled than others.

Meanwhile, there is no perfect way to read the Bible. There are countless aids available to help the reader make sense of the Scriptures, it is just the case of finding the right one that works for you.

Here are two invaluable pieces of advice I have picked up along the way to help me in all of this. Firstly, when on holiday, I try something different. With the usual daily routine broken, on my last holiday I downloaded Nicky Gumbel's Bible in One Year app and found my Bible and prayer times to be as refreshing as the break itself as a result. Secondly, when something isn't working anymore, change it. There is nothing wrong with changing a routine in order to keep your prayer life and Bible reading fresh and energised.

Suggestions

- Take a look at the various apps or online tools to see if there is anything out there that might help you in your prayer and Bible study.

- Never be afraid to change things in order to 'freshen up' your daily prayer as Bible study.

- If you have never prayed using the carefully thought-out words of other people, then let the richness to be found in such prayers invigorate your prayer life.

Questions

- Have you made a commitment to daily prayer, worship and Bible study?

- Are there others you could join with at your local church who would encourage you in these matters?

- Are there colleagues in your workplace who you could join together with to pray?

- What works for you / what really isn't helpful?

2. Church

I will make a weekly commitment to attend church and participate fully in church life.

(Let us) not give up meeting together, as some are in the habit of doing, but encouraging one another....

HEBREWS 10:25

There's nothing like the local church when it's working right. Its beauty is indescribable.

Its power is breathtaking.

Bill Hybels

I have met plenty of people who would consider themselves to be 'ok' with God but wouldn't dream of setting foot in a church. Organised religion is not for them, in fact they say it does more harm than good. I have a lot a sympathy with people who are sceptical about church because so often we have got things drastically wrong. But then what can you expect? Each and every church is simply a gathering of broken people who have an amazing capacity to do good and yet at the same time make many mistakes.

In my 30+ years as a Christian I have belonged to six different churches. I have had good times in each one of them but I have also been disappointed at times by my fellow believers along the way; disheartened by what I have seen and heard. But the reality is I am a stronger, more faith-filled, more mature Christian because of those churches. I have heard it described as being like stones in a washing machine....

Now I know it really wouldn't be a very good idea to put a load of stones into a washing machine and turn on the spin. But what would happen if you did? Assuming the machine could withstand the battering it would take, as the stones tumbled together, all the rough edges would be knocked off and the stones would become smooth. Through the banging against each other, they would change and would become more beautiful. This wonderfully depicts what happens in a church seeking to function together as God's people. As we bang against each other, our rough edges get knocked off; we become smoother, more rounded, easier to handle.

All of us have sharp edges. Recognising this in the context of other believers and being willing to be re-shaped by and with them is a beautiful thing, if a little painful at times. When church works well, it is also very attractive to those on the outside looking in, who can perhaps see transformation in lives taking place.

I am a passionate believer in the local church. Yes it can be messy, broken and even dysfunctional at times but when it works well, there is nothing on this earth that can touch it. A great church can be the means by which personal and societal change can take place - and we need both in our world today. The local church is the hope of the world.[5]

I suggest that a Christian's commitment to their local church should be regular and wholehearted. It is so easy today to treat church as we would our leisure activities. We attend when it suits us or when we feel like it and conversely when we get a better offer or we are feeling demotivated, our attendance lapses.

Without doubt, those of us in church leadership must share the responsibility for changes in the patterns of attendance. In 2000, respected British theologian, John Drane, wrote a book called The McDonaldization of the Church. In it, he identified a trend that churches were

---

[5] This can be heard most years at the Willow Creek Association Global Leadership Summit.

becoming stereotyped structures, offering uninventive pre-packaged worship. Too many churches were following a set formula and running the risk of squeezing out God in the process. If this was or still is the case, then it might be due to the fact that to an increasing degree church-goers see themselves as consumers. As a consumer, if my church is not offering me what I like or want, then I will simply go down the road to another or maybe even stop going at all. The success of the McDonalds fast food chain is built around the fact that you know exactly what you are going to get regardless of which branch you go into. Church should not be like this, primarily because we are not 'consumers' of church, we are the church and as the Body of Christ we have the privilege of joining in with God's activity in the world. Truly understand that and our casual approach to gathering together each week will surely change.

Much of what we do together as a Church, can be done individually but when we do it together, as a community of believers, we experience something of God and his presence that is different, almost unique. Of course, churches differ one from another, but most would include the following in their weekly gathering:

A.   Worship - The Westminster Catechism poses (and answers) this interesting question: What is the chief end of man? The answer is it is to glorify God, and to enjoy him forever.[6] Worship (of God) is our reason for being. When we worship God, we are doing the thing we were primarily created to do. This is not to deny that worship has some other consequences or benefits but they are secondary. Sung worship (note that worship doesn't have to be 'sung') can be engaged in alone but when experienced with others can be a wonderfully uplifting experience. God is glorified and we are encouraged - almost reason enough to make a regular commitment to church attendance! But once again, this is secondary; if it does the community or us good then wonderful, but worship is for God since he is worth it.

B.   Teaching / Preaching / Expounding the word of God - to listen to someone explain God's word from the Bible is a humbling experience. It is also quite counter-cultural in this day and age to give your time and attention to someone sharing in this way. That is not to say we should receive what is said without questioning or deliberation, for each of us has been given the ability to think for ourselves and truly wrestle with the word of God. But what a gift it is to listen to a preacher who has, each week, studied, prayed and poured over the passage set before them. And how arrogant we

---

[6] 'The Westminster Shorter Catechism', in The Presbyterian Church (USA) *Book of Confessions* (Louisville, Ky: Office of the General Assembly, 1983), Q.1.

risk being when we say we don't need this for our spiritual growth and nourishment.

C.   Eucharist - just about every Christian denomination and church around the world recognises the importance of the gathered community breaking bread and sharing wine together as the Lord himself directed. See the next chapter for a fuller explanation of this.

D.   Prayer and Intercession - as already outlined in chapter 1, prayer is a crucially important activity for the follower of Christ. But when believers gather to intercede together, not unlike worship, another dimension is added. Corporate prayer can take many and varied forms but there is great power in agreeing in prayer and collectively seeking God for answers or wisdom or breakthrough. I never lead a church service without some form of corporate prayer with the Lord's Prayer being as good a place as any to start.

E.   Empowering - The final part of the Prayer of Thanksgiving that forms the last part of the Church of England Communion liturgy, is as follows:

Send us out in the power of the Holy Spirit,
to live and work to your praise and glory.

This is such a timely reminder that all the elements of our weekly church gathering that we engage in, somehow prepare us (or should) to live as followers of Christ outside of that building. We are to be an outward-looking people, keen not to keep the knowledge of the love of God to ourselves but to share it, by all means, and with all people. We are the church, not the bricks and mortar that we gather in once a week (or more) to worship, listen, intercede and break bread. And we are that church 24/7 in our homes, workplaces, communities and schools. I firmly believe that. But I also believe that the hour (or more) that we commit to spending together in that funny-shaped building at the end of the street is the most important hour we spend all week. It is where we are nurtured, fed, challenged, encouraged and it is where we get to undertake the activity we are made firstly to do - glorify God. It is not perfect (it can't be for I am part of it) but it is a glimpse of heaven and I for one wouldn't want to live without it.

At 5pm today, I rang our church bell to signal the beginning of Evening Prayer - the daily gathering mentioned in the previous chapter. As I sat down, it quickly became apparent that tonight I was on my own. For one reason or another my regular Evening Prayer comrades were unable to join me today, which reminded me just how precious a gift it is to belong to a worshipping community. Don't get me wrong, some of my most memorable times in God's presence have been spent alone in church buildings but how much easier it is, more fulfilling, to join with other like-minded (generally) believers to worship, pray, listen and meditate. Thank you God for each fellow-member of my worshipping community and for what I experience and learn of you through them.

Suggestions

- Make a regular and consistent commitment to a local church that broadly shares your beliefs and values.

- Ask God to reveal something of himself to you through the practices and traditions that perhaps haven't formed part of your experience to date.

- Check your attitude before you enter through the door on Sunday morning. Be open and generous as well as whole-hearted.

Questions

- How can you best encourage those tasked with leading your church?

- Do you have unrealistic expectations of your church community?

- What is stopping you from making a weekly one-hour commitment to meeting together with other believers?

3. Eucharist

I will consistently take bread and wine within the Body of Christ as a reminder that Christ died for me.

This is my body, which is for you;
do this in remembrance of me.
1 CORINTHIANS 11:24

The purpose of the Lord's Supper is to receive from Christ the nourishment and strength and hope and joy that come from feasting our souls on all that He purchased for us on the cross, especially His own fellowship.

John Piper

There is nothing I love more than sitting round a table with trusted friends enjoying good food and drink. Time seems to fly by and evenings often seem way too short as the conversation flows. Jesus seemed particularly keen on this too, in fact it is incredible just how much of his ministry was conducted in the informal setting of a meal table.[7]

The gospel writers record one such event for us the night before Jesus' crucifixion. He and his closest friends were gathered in an upper room in Jerusalem to celebrate the Passover Festival; a meal that was in itself a tangible reminder that God had delivered their ancestors out of slavery in Egypt approximately 1500 years earlier. As the meal neared its end, Jesus took two of its most basic components and gave them a whole new meaning for every generation that would follow.

And he took bread, gave thanks and broke it, and gave it to them, saying, 'This is my body given for you; do this in remembrance of me.' In the same way, after the supper he took the cup, saying, 'This cup is the new covenant in my blood, which is poured out for you.'

LUKE 22:19-20

The precise meaning of Jesus' words would have been beyond the disciples' comprehension and have in fact exercised Christians ever since. For centuries, the Church has grappled with both what He meant and what

---

[7] For a detailed exploration of this topic, try Conrad Gempf's excellent book: 'Mealtime Habits of the Messiah'.

legitimate meaning we can attach to the act of consuming the same elements of bread and wine today.

I grew up in a church that had a separate Communion Service every Sunday. Rooted in the Brethren tradition, often no-one officially 'led' the service, instead the bread and wine acted as the centre-piece of the gathering and different congregation members contributed as they felt led by God. This was an 'Act of Remembrance' as no real significance was attached to the bread and wine except for what they symbolised. We used a bread roll that you might have for your tea and sparkling grape juice (red, thankfully) that you would be just as likely to use as an accompaniment to Sunday lunch.

Since then, my personal understanding of what happens when we take bread and wine together as God's people has developed somewhat over the years and as such it remains a key part of my worship as a follower of Christ. Now, as an Anglican priest, I have the privilege of leading people through Eucharistic liturgy that is multi-faceted in nature and rich in content.

The Eucharist[8] is one of the Sacraments of the Church[9],

---

[8] Also referred to as Communion, the Lord's Supper, the Breaking of Bread and Mass.

[9] When the 39 Articles were accepted by Anglicans generally as a norm for Anglican teaching, they recognised two sacraments as having been ordained by Christ: Baptism and Eucharist , to which, broadly speaking, Catholics add a further five: Confirmation, Confession, Anointing the sick, Marriage and Ordination.

meaning it is a means of God's grace to His people. It is an external sign of an inward reality. Where would we be without outward signs to express what is taking place inside of us. A kiss on the cheek, a wave of the hand, a hug, a 'thumbs-up' are just a few of the physical actions we use to communicate something going on inside. And so on this Passover night, rich in symbolism in and of itself, we find Jesus taking two everyday common components, bread and wine, and attaching hugely significant meaning to their consumption. As a result, when we follow the command of Jesus to break bread in this way, we firstly get to look back, we secondly focus on His presence here today, and thirdly we look forward.

Looking back

> 'Do this in remembrance of me.'
> LUKE 22:19

I know how easy it could be for me to become blasé about the death of Jesus - to take it for granted. Regular breaking of bread helps me guard against this and forces me to stop and reflect on this incredible life-changing moment.

It does all of us good to bring His sacrifice to mind. As we reflect upon Christ's suffering, it surely strengthens us to resist temptation and flee from the sin that nailed him to the cross.[10]

---

[10] As song-writer Stuart Townend put it in *How Deep the Father's Love For Us* - 'It was my sin that held him there, until it was accomplished'.

Without the cross, we are lost. Without the death and resurrection of Jesus, we are stuck in our sin without hope of reconciliation with God.[11] Every time we take bread and wine we are taken back to Christ's broken body and his shed blood; and we have the opportunity to respond in praise, in wonder and in worship.

Nourishment today

In the first few weeks of my Church of England curacy I had the pleasure of meeting a vicar who had been 40 years in the job. I asked him what had sustained him during his long years of ministry. Unsurprisingly he said his practice of Morning and Evening Prayer was key. But further to this, I then learnt (from his Curate) that he had celebrated the Eucharist everyday for those 40 years. Usually with a group of others but occasionally alone, he had found nourishment and sustenance in the daily routine of eating bread and drinking wine. For him it was truly life-giving.

And so it is that the Eucharist does not just look back to a past event or look forward to an age that is to come, but it is also a meal for today. In celebrating the Eucharist, we are held secure between the past and the future.

This is not the place to debate just how Jesus is present

---

[11] For God was pleased to have all his fullness dwell in him, and through him to reconcile to himself all things, whether things on earth or things in heaven, by making peace through his blood, shed on the cross. Colossians 1:19-20.

at the communion table. For me, the key phrase we use in the Anglican liturgy comes as part of the Eucharistic Prayer:

> "As we proclaim his death and celebrate his rising in glory, send your Holy Spirit that this bread and this wine may be to us the body and blood of your dear Son."

Having prayed that prayer, in faith we believe that in some mystical sense, simple bread and wine are transformed for/in consumption, and as they are consumed they nourish and sustain the recipient. In the same way that bread nourishes the body for life, this 'spiritual' bread nourishes us for our spiritual life.[12] In some inexplicable way, we get to feed on Jesus. And in that present day moment, in a life often full of complexity and confusion, a fresh, life-sustaining encounter with the risen Jesus Christ occurs that re-energises us and compels us to live that same risen life.

Looking forward

And there is more. Not only is this a present day meal with a focus on a once-and-forever life-changing event, it also points us forward to what is to come.

Approximately 2000 years ago, God's future arrived in the present in the person of Jesus. In Him we see a glimpse of what God's new world will be like in the new

---

[12] I actually dislike the distinction between 'life' and 'spiritual life'. They are one; everything is spiritual.

heaven and the new earth that will be created.[13] This new order will be an entirely physical experience as well as a spiritual one and Jesus will be right at the centre of it.[14] When this happens every longing of our hearts will be satisfied by His presence and His love. Until that time comes, we have the Eucharist as a kind of foretaste of what is to come. In the same way that the Holy Spirit is the 'down-payment' or guarantee of our inheritance[15] so it is with the bread and wine. The food and drink we share in the Eucharist speak uniquely of the presence of Jesus and the words that accompany the meal are a declaration of his coming.

"For whenever you eat this bread and drink this cup, you proclaim the Lord's death until he comes."

1 CORINTHIANS 11:26

The food and drink we share in love with one another is a foretaste, a picture of what we shall share together for all eternity. We shall enjoy the company of one another and of God who will of course, be at the centre of all that we do.

I talked at greater length about what it means to be 'Church' in the previous chapter. The Eucharist is the epitome of this - the epicentre of community. Using

---

[13] Revelation 21

[14] See Luke 24 and John 20-21 for a glimpse of Jesus' resurrected body.

[15] Ephesians 1:13-14

beautiful words created centuries ago, when we gather together in this way, we get to make peace with God and with each other; we confess our sins and ask forgiveness of God and each other. It is a profound and beautiful thing.

This key part of Christian worship takes different forms in different denominational structures. But one thing the Apostle Paul does make clear is a warning against coming to take bread and wine flippantly or in an inappropriate manner.

So then, whoever eats the bread or drinks the cup of the Lord in an unworthy manner will be guilty of sinning against the body and blood of the Lord. Everyone ought to examine themselves before they eat of the bread and drink from the cup. For those who eat and drink without discerning the body of Christ eat and drink judgment on themselves. 1 CORINTHIANS 11:27-29

This is a holy act and should not be undertaken lightly or casually but at the same time, it is also a celebration. Some churches certainly know how to party and many members revel in using their gift of hospitality. It is also true that some churches have little concept of this and need to learn how to celebrate God's goodness. As His creatures, I believe we are made to celebrate - primarily our good God. The Eucharist is a celebratory meal joining together the past event, the present moment and the future that is to come. And as such, it is an important part of my simple Rule of Life.

Suggestions

- The next time you share the Eucharist, take a moment to reflect that as you do so you are joining in with Christians from all around the world in every denomination who are doing the same thing.

- Find when churches located near where you live or work have a midweek / lunchtime Eucharist and plan it into your schedule.

Questions

- Does the Eucharist form part of your regular worship pattern? If not, why not?

- Have you considered celebrating the Eucharist in a church with a different tradition to that which you are used to? It might broaden your experience of God.

4. Good Emotional Health

I will make an on-going commitment to think well and co-operate with God's plan for transformation in my life.

Be transformed by the renewing of your mind.
ROMANS 12:2

The way we live will inevitably be a reflection of the way we think. True change always begins in our mind.
John Ortberg

How much consideration do any of us give to the unhelpful, distracting and potentially destructive thought patterns and processes that live and thrive inside our heads? At best, they might be described as 'unproductive' and consequently they sap us of mental (and physical) energy. At worst, they can eat us up from within, changing our mood, attitude and ultimately our behaviour markedly. After 30+ years of being a Christian, I am increasingly convinced that we need to pay attention to what is going on in our heads and make a serious commitment to health and wholeness in our thinking. I believe this to be one of the keys to unlocking God's transformative work in our lives - transformation that is for our benefit and His glory. Personal experience tells me that this is very much an on-going process, not a one-off life event.

It used to be believed that little change went on in a person's brain once it was fully formed. But more recently, a dramatic increase in understanding of what are called 'neurological pathways' has changed all that. Just as a shortcut across a grassy area becomes more pronounced with use, so these pathways in the brain become more established as they are used. Similarly, they diminish when not in use. All of this leads to the conclusion that we really can change the way we think! As these good and bad thinking pathways are changing all the time, we actually get to invest in the healthiness of our own brain.

John Ortberg writes: "Even twenty years ago, researchers

thought the adult brain was genetically determined and structurally unchangeable. But they have since found that even into adulthood the brain is amazingly changeable - it has neuroplasticity. Which synapses remain and which ones wither away depends on your mental habits. Those that carry no traffic go out of business like bus routes with no customers. Those that get heavily trafficked get stronger and thicker. The mind shapes the brain."[16]

Imagine a work colleague ignores your jovial morning greeting because they are lost in their thoughts about a worrying situation at home. Except you know nothing of their domestic situation and instead choose to interpret it as a snub and evidence that they really do not like you. Fuelled by that belief, you then begin to over analyse every look or exchange you have with them and you quickly decide you have done something awful to offend them and you are definitely off their Christmas card list! And yet when you buck up enough courage to confront them about it all, ready to apologise for the offence you have clearly caused you are met with surprise and confusion because no such offence exists. The thought patterns are thriving in your brain along an increasingly established neural pathway and yet the whole thing is a complete fabrication - alive only in your head.

On-going

In this chapter's key verse from Romans 12:2, the Greek

---

[16] John Ortberg, The Me I Want To Be, p. 97

words we translate as conform and transform are present passive imperatives indicating the continuing nature of Paul's instruction. In other words, the renewal of the mind[17] and resulting transformation is not a one-off event but, rather, on-going. This needs to happen again and again and keep on happening. This is a lifetime's work, not a tick-box exercise, which goes a long way to explain why I have made part of my Rule of Life a commitment to good emotional health. In the world of the 'quick-fix', the renewal of the mind is not a one-off event to be ticked off or recorded in some sort of 'spiritual log-book'. None other than the great German reformer Martin Luther said "the renewal of the mind....takes place from day to day and progresses farther and farther."[18] The Apostle Paul recognised this in his own life:

Though outwardly we are wasting away,
yet inwardly we are being renewed day-by-day.

2 CORINTHIANS 4:16

And a few chapters later, he is very practical; he gives the reader something to do:

We demolish arguments and every pretension that sets itself up against the knowledge of God, and we take captive every thought to make it obedient to Christ.

2 CORINTHIANS 10:5

---

[17] This is the phrase that St Paul uses. It would appear he was talking about ways/patterns of thinking rather than the chemical/physical changes we now know are possible.

[18] Martin Luther, *Commentary on Romans*, p. 168

Paul clearly believes that the renewal of the mind is possible and that through discipline, choice and surrender, old patterns of thinking can be replaced by new.

I suggest that what might loosely be called 'bad thinking' can perhaps be broken down into three areas:

1. Thinking about God.

2. Thinking about other people.

3. Thinking about ourselves.

A flawed or false view of God quickly damages our relationship with Him and our ability to live as followers of Christ. If we think He is angry and vengeful or even disinterested and distant, then how we pray to Him or worship Him will clearly be negatively impacted.[19] If you spend your whole time thinking your neighbour is your enemy who hates you and wants to cause you harm, then that will massively affect your friendships and relationships. Your life will be dominated by fear and you will increasingly withdraw and live a reclusive life.

Finally, we must develop the ability or have the discipline to view ourselves as God sees us. We are neither God (thankfully!) nor nothing. Each one of us is precious and valuable to God as well as being uniquely created by

---

[19] If you are tempted to think that way then read Luke 11:11-13 & 15: 11-32 as a reminder that God is a loving Father who has good gifts for you.

Him. Given our propensity as sinners to be so self-consumed, it is so very easy to get this one wrong.

What are we to think?

Allowing the Spirit of God to renew the mind and thinking well as a discipline is not just about what NOT to think but also about what you DO think about. It concerns what comes IN as well as what you keep OUT. Paul makes this very point in writing to the Church in Philippi:

Finally, brothers and sisters, whatever is true, whatever is noble, whatever is right, whatever is pure, whatever is lovely, whatever is admirable—if anything is excellent or praiseworthy—think about such things.
PHILIPPIANS 4:8

Every single day we are bombarded by the insistent messages of the world that seek to shape and influence our thinking about God, each other and ourselves.[20] Who are you listening to? We need to be soaked in the word of God in order to get His perspective on life's challenges and joys. This is one of the reasons why my commitment to the Daily Office is in place. The picture painted in Psalm 1 is one of renewal, transformation and nourishment by the word of God.

(Blessed is the one) whose delight is in the law of the

---

[20] Subliminal messages like "God's not real", "that culture is dangerous" or "you must look like this to be happy".

Lord, and who meditates on his law day and night.
PSALM 1:2

Taboo

Having mental health issues remains a huge taboo in many Christian circles and this should not be the case. The Apostle Paul wrote a huge amount about the importance of sound thinking in his New Testament letters, often adding a personal perspective, and yet he isn't regarded as fragile or unspiritual by New Testament historians. Here is one example:

> For in my inner being I delight in God's law; but I see another law at work in me, waging war against the law of my mind and making me a prisoner of the law of sin at work within me.
> ROMANS 7:22-23

There is undoubtedly a battle going on in our minds because sin and self, although eternally defeated on the Cross, are still real and relevant in this age.

In 2014, a hugely 'successful'[21] church leader and pastor, Steven Furtick wrote: "I've got this ceaseless war going on inside my heart and my head. I'm waging it every millisecond of every minute of every hour of every

---

[21] At least as many people would define success. At the age of 34 he leads Elevation Church in Moncks Corner, South Carolina, the church he founded, which has a regular weekly attendance of 18,000 people. He has also written two New York Times best seller books, has a wife and three children.

day."[22] Asking for help in this area is not a sign of weakness but is actually the courageous thing to do. If you are stuck in a certain way of thinking that you simply cannot break free from and you know it is stopping your transformation into the person God intends you to be, then help is at hand. A friend or family member could help you take the first step. A counsellor or other professional could help bring the desired breakthrough. As someone alive to the realities of spiritual warfare, a church leader would definitely be worth speaking to.

We may be on the road to sanctification but it is a long and winding one and there is still a way to travel yet. Not every thought can be trusted.

God knows

To begin the process of self-examination is maybe daunting and potentially alarming, however it is vital for good emotional health. It is a scary thing to begin to see the truth about your own mind; to peer into the dark places and see the need for its cleansing or healing. Far easier to ignore, disguise or pretend that those places either do not exist or are not that dark at all. But God is not surprised by what has been previously hidden. The Psalmist writes:

> You have searched me, LORD, and you know me.
> You know when I sit and when I rise;

---

[22] Steven Furtick, *Crash the Chatterbox*, Loc. 149

you perceive my thoughts from afar.

PSALM 139:1-2

God not only knows our thoughts better than we do but He also knows them before we have even had them! It takes courage and perseverance to allow our minds to be renewed and it is potentially painful along the way. But the result is the classic hallmark of Christians increasingly becoming more like their Saviour:

You will keep in perfect peace those whose minds are steadfast, because they trust in you.

ISAIAH 26:3

In tune

On 30 July 1967, a young 17-year-old woman misjudged the depth of the water diving into Chesapeake Bay, Maryland, USA. The accident left her permanently paralysed from the shoulders down. Writing about Joni Eareckson Tada, Bill Hybels said, "she knows how to live life so tuned in (to) the Holy Spirit that His voice merges with her inner voice; His view of the world becomes her view as well. She has learned how to drown out fear's whispers in favour of adopting God's take on any given situation."[23] Given her new found circumstances, here was a woman whose life seemed destined to be marked by anger, regret, despair and perhaps depression. But Hybels' description of Eareckson Tada is entirely congruous with Romans 12:2. It is exactly how one might

23 Bill Hybels, *Axiom,* Loc. 2741

expect a 'renewed mind' to manifest itself. Her body may have been rendered largely nonfunctional nearly 50 years ago but since then (and probably before) her mind has been continually renewed such that she is visibly 'in tune' with the Holy Spirit according to one of the key leaders of this age.

Choice

Each one of us has a choice: we really are free to decide what our mind will dwell on and what it will jettison as useless or harmful. The choice is to submit to the will of God, have Him renew our mind and consequently transform our life or to stay in the shadows where the lies of the enemy induce fear and restrict God's work in our life. Fear is one of the Christian's biggest enemies. It restricts, disables and ultimately defeats Christians in their pursuit of God's good purposes for them. Bill Hybels says, "You can bring order and discipline to your thinking by surrendering your fears to the power of Jesus Christ."[24]

As part of my Rule of Life, I make an on-going commitment to co-operate with the Spirit of God in His work to renew my mind, maintain good emotional health and bring about transformation. In 1 Corinthians 2:16, Paul says 'We have the mind of Christ.' That promise should spark in us a prayer that we might trade our ordinary human consciousness for something of the

---

[24] Bill Hybels, Simplify. Ten Practices to Unclutter Your Soul, p. 157

knowledge and insight of God himself. Thinking 'God thoughts' is within our reach!

Suggestions

- Carve out some time to sit and consider what you believe about God, other people and yourself.

- Consider keeping a journal so you can see the positive changes taking place in your life over time.

- Identify a few things that you know do you good emotionally / mentally and make sure you are doing them!

Questions

- Who or what is shaping your mindset at the beginning of each day?

- Is it time for some 'emotional gardening' in your life? Pruning? Digging up? Planting?

- Would you know where to turn for help in this area?

5. Care for the Physical Body

I will take responsibility for my physical health and well-being, primarily through a focus on diet and exercise.

Do you not know that your bodies are temples of the Holy Spirit, who is in you, whom you have received from God?

1 CORINTHIANS 6:19

Your body is holy because God made it, and everything God makes has a purpose. We are to bring glory to God with our bodies.

Rick Warren

Having looked at good emotional health in the previous chapter, we now turn our attention to wider health issues with particular reference to the health of the physical body. This topic falls into a category that Jesus did not have a great deal to say on directly but nonetheless we will draw on plenty of Biblical resources to help and inform us.

In my previous church we had an evening service which draws many people who find themselves on the fringes or margins of society. For a disproportionate number of the regulars, their bodies bare the scars of abuse - some of it suffered at the hands of others, much of it self-inflicted. Some have battled alcohol and/or substance abuse for years and look disheveled, unkempt or beaten up (sometimes literally) as a result. As I write, Tony (not his real name) comes to mind. He has a look of desperation in his eyes that cries out to you and says "I'm trapped, help me." He confesses that he "drinks alcoholically" just to get him through the day. Drink and drugs are at one end of the spectrum but for many of us, our vice is much more everyday: sugar. Levels of over-eating and obesity are at epidemic levels as we are bombarded by tempting sugary treats at supermarket checkouts, petrol stations and coffee shops. You cannot even go to a Post Office to buy a stamp without having to make the decision as to whether to have a Mars Bar with it! So does it really matter and if so, what can I do to honour God by caring for my physical body?

My body belongs to God

Firstly, it is important to remember that your body is not your own, it actually belongs to God.

'I have the right to do anything,' you say – but not everything is beneficial. 'I have the right to do anything'– but I will not be mastered by anything. You say, 'Food for the stomach and the stomach for food, and God will destroy them both.' The body, however, is not meant for sexual immorality but for the Lord, and the Lord for the body. By his power God raised the Lord from the dead, and he will raise us also. Do you not know that your bodies are members of Christ himself?
1 CORINTHIANS 6:12-15

God created us, He breathed life into us - we owe everything we have and all that we are, to Him. No created thing in this world would survive and thrive without the Creator and Sustainer. Therefore decisions about what we do with/to our bodies are not ours alone to make. They are to be made in conjunction with and for the glory of God.

All of me is precious to God

Many people have great trouble in believing they are precious to God; that He loves them. Further to this, those who have at some level accepted this truth about God believe that He is really only interested in their inner being - their soul or spirit and that their body is of little or no interest to Him. This is a common misconception with a rather more Gnostic[25] basis than a Biblical one.

Such thinking rejects the importance of the human body and of the material world or cosmos. Dualism is evident in setting up Material (or Matter) versus Spiritual (or Soul); Spiritual being good and material being bad. When this kind of thinking creeps in, it leads us to believe that God is only interested in the soul whereas the rest of us is unimportant and will be destroyed. There are three counter arguments to this.

1)   God created both body and soul so who are we to say that one is unimportant to Him?

2)   The book of Revelation tells us that one day God will create a New Heaven and a New Earth.[26] The picture this book paints is of an entirely physical existence, in some respects not unlike the one we experience now. Also, what we read of the earth that God created before the Fall[27] is quite possibly a good indication of what the New Heaven and Earth will one day look like and that too is a physical world.

3)   When God came to earth in the person of His Son

---

[25] Gnosticism (from Ancient Greek: "having knowledge") is a modern term to include a variety of ancient religions, originating in the first and second century.

[26] Revelation 21

[27] In Genesis chapters 1 & 2

Jesus, He came not as a disembodied spirit but as flesh and blood.

We are entirely precious to God - all of us! The parts we can see, feel and touch, as well as that part of us that lives on after this earthly body has gone.

God's Spirit lives in me

When we put our faith and trust in Jesus Christ as Lord and Saviour, the Holy Spirit comes and lives within us. At that point we carry a very precious cargo and as such the vessel or body in which the Spirit lives has a very important role.

One day God will resurrect my body

I have already made the point that when God came to earth he chose to come as flesh and blood, in bodily form. Furthermore, when Christ conquered death and rose again, he was resurrected in bodily form. His body may have been slightly different to the earlier model, but it was physical.[28] What we see in the Biblical accounts of Jesus' resurrected body is a glimpse of what our resurrected bodies will also look like.

Having understood that our earthly bodies are important to God, precious to Him even, then an on-going commitment to take care of our earthly body should logically follow. This is why I have this principle in my Rule

---

[28] In John 21 we read that the risen Jesus cooked and shared breakfast with his disciples on the Galilee shore.

of Life and here are some thoughts as to how one might look after our bodies.

Identify your rhythms

As God's created beings, we flourish when we identify and live by healthy patterns or rhythms of living.

- Sleep - sleep is your body's way of recovering after the activities of the day. Work out how much sleep you need in order to thrive and not just survive. Switch off mobile devices and anything likely to disrupt sleep (with apologies to those with young children who you cannot switch off - I've been there!) because quality of sleep is as important as quantity.

Some smartphones have a bedtime function that tell you when to go to bed and when to get up. It is suggested that going to bed and waking up at the same time every day are keys to healthy sleep.

- Sabbath - we are designed to rest one day in every seven. I develop this much further in chapter 7.

- Holidays - the working / resting balance should be extended beyond the weekly principle. I plan my time off a year in advance which helps my mind and body pace itself through peak times of activity.

Establish good habits

Having identified and established a good short and medium term rhythm to life, good habits must then be in place to sit alongside this. Classic 'self-help' theories suggest that positive new habits can be established in 21-28 days[29], but let us not get too focused on how long it takes but rather be encouraged that habits can be changed - especially those around diet and exercise.

1) Diet - I can recognise periods in my own adult life when my eating habits have had good positive effects on my body and negative or harmful ones. There is undoubtedly a plethora of books out there on this topic and I don't intend to add to it. Suffice to say, the recommended daily intake of calories per day for a man/woman is approximately 2,500/2,000[30] and 5, 7 or 10 (depending on who you believe) portions of fruit/veg a day will do you good.[31]

2) Exercise - again, there's nothing new here, you've heard it all before. Eating a balanced diet combined with taking regular exercise are the two very best things you can do to maintain good physical (and incidentally mental) health. The American College of Sports Medicine (ACSM)[32] is

---

[29] Check out this article for an alternative viewpoint: https://www.theguardian.com/lifeandstyle/2009/oct/10/change-your-life-habit-28-day-rule

[30] http://www.nhs.uk/chq/pages/1126.aspx?categoryid=51

[31] http://www.nhs.uk/news/2014/04april/pages/five-a-day-should-be-upped-to-seven-a-day.aspx

[32] http://www.acsm.org

the largest sports medicine and exercise science organisation in the world. It's recommended guidelines are 150 minutes of moderate intensity exercise per week.[33]

Choice

This seems like a good point to remind you, the reader, of a key principle that under-pins the entire Rule of Life - you have the choice! No-one is forcing change upon us, rather each of us has the choice as to whether we want to implement these changes in our life or not. We can choose to be the people we want to be by choosing daily practices that will help bring change about. But we are not alone....

1.   God's power not just will-power - we are not on our own in this, God is with us! When we have identified, prayerfully before God, certain lifestyle choices or changes that would help us become the people that He wants us to be, then He will be with us, helping us through the process. He makes the resources of heaven available to us and let us never forget that God's Spirit lives within us as our constant guide, companion and helper.

2.   In chapter 2 we looked at the benefits of belonging to the church, the community of God's people. Never more so than when we are being

---

[33] = 30-60 mins moderate exercise 5 days a week or 20-60 mins rigorous intensity exercise 3x a week.

challenged and changed. To give something up (like chocolate!) or start something new (like going to the gym) is extremely hard but can be made easier when friends are around you to encourage and support you. Accountability is rapidly going out of fashion in a world where freedom equates to doing what you want. But having someone or a small group of people who will ask you how you are doing in your commitment to do / not do something is incredibly powerful and motivational. Such a group doesn't just have to provide accountability but also prayer support and a 'listening ear' or 'arm round the shoulder' when set-backs occur.

Commitment to good emotional health and care for the physical body are closely linked. We can be confident that developing good habits and leaving behind unhealthy ones is possible, especially if neurological pathways are flexible (see previous chapter). This starts in the mind. I am very much a 'work in progress' in this area (and all the others to be honest) but my commitment to keep working at it, with the help of God's Spirit, remains undiminished.

Suggestions

- Do not confuse your identity with your (old) habits.

- Read Ephesians 4:22-24. Consider what (in this area) you might 'put off' and indeed 'put on'.

- Share your plans for change with trusted friends - ask for help and support.

- Drink more water / Eat off smaller plates / Take a walk everyday.

Questions

- Do you know in your heart that you (all of you!) are precious to God?

- Do you have an identifiable rhythm to your day / week / month or term / year?

- What achievable small steps could you implement straight away in pursuit of change?

- Can you identify people who you can trust who will help you walk this path?

6. Friends and Family

I will consistently spend quality time with the people who are most important to me.

A friend loves at all times,
and a brother is born for a time of adversity.
PROVERBS 17:17

Yesterday has gone, tomorrow has not yet come.
We have only today. Let us begin.
Mother Teresa

The absolute key in developing a working Rule of Life and finding a rhythm that honours God is resisting busyness. We simply have to stop and take a step back and make a commitment to ensuring that our diaries truly reflect the important things in our life. What is most important to me beyond my on-going relationship with God (from which everything else flows) is my relationships with the people I love. My wife, my children, my extended family and my friends are all gifts from God to me and I make it my desire to love and cherish them. How do I do that? Well, I give them the most precious gift I can - my time.

My diary is full - I don't say that with any sense of pride, in fact it is a pet-hate of mine when people tell you how busy they are because they believe that busy people are important people. I block everything out in my electronic diary so that it is clear just where I am meant to be at any particular point of the week and what I am going to be doing when I get there. In theory my phone bleeps with an 'Alert' to remind me of what is coming up thus ensuring I am not late. But the first two items that go in the diary, that highlight where my priorities lie are a 24-hour Sabbath (see the next chapter) and a date night with my wife. Alongside time with my boys, other appointments then build up the look of the week until, as I say, it looks quite full. But the key is, there is rhythm and balance and always time for the people I love.

Allow me to take an important detour for one moment before I get back to family, friends and the problem of busyness. I dispensed with 'to do' lists some time ago and it is one of the best decisions I have ever made. If a task is important then it goes straight into my calendar with an allotted time slot. If it is not important, then it should not be appearing on a 'to do' list anyway! Such lists only serve as a reminder of all the work you have yet to do or all the tasks you didn't get done. Once you have scheduled an appropriate time slot in your calendar for a particular task, then you can forget about it until that slot comes. This works brilliantly for me with the key to the whole plan being to actually complete the task when you have scheduled to do so. In your mind, you need to treat it like any other appointment in your calendar. So for instance, you would not think of missing a doctors appointment and bumping it the next day simply because you did not feel like going. That same attitude and practice must be adopted to the tasks you schedule in your calendar.[34]

Some may ask, 'What's wrong with being busy? Isn't it just the way life is now?' The truth is, society pushes us to the limits of our time, resources and energy so we can do more, achieve more and contribute more. One problem is that the requests on our time are often to do really good and honourable things. In my previous church we hosted a community hub for homeless and disadvantaged people in our premises but I did not

---

[34] I had adopted this approach to task completion long before I read Kevin Kruse's excellent book, *15 Secrets Successful People Know About Time Management*. But he gets credit elsewhere!

attend it in the three years I was there. Part of the issue was that it took place on my Sabbath but also I simply chose to make decisions about what to be involved in and what to leave to others. It was a brilliant project - but in that period it was not for me to be involved in. The truth is if we say 'yes' to every opportunity or request then there will be a huge price to pay. Often we find ourselves too busy for unhurried / meaningful conversations with special, important people. We hold good intentions but never seem to be able to act on them and we consume a diet of guilt as a result. We are just too busy to nurture existing relationships let alone foster new ones. We regularly fail to look after ourselves as we would wish (see chapter 5) typically through lack of sleep or absence of exercise. And, of course, God gets squeezed out too. We find no time to rest in His presence, to listen to Him, wait upon Him or develop intimacy with Him. Also, the reality is we often talk about the problem as if the 'spirit of busyness' has visited us in the night and left a deposit with us. And now there is nothing we can do about it. But there is! We can slay the dragon of busyness and we must ruthlessly eliminate hurry from our lives.

Some times our over-activity (often work) has at its heart a desire to provide security for ourselves and our loved ones (Have you ever heard it said, 'I'm only doing this for the family'?). But our security should come from a trust in God who is always faithful and never lets us down. Then there is the problem of seeking approval from those around us. We live as if life is one big episode of 'Britain's Got Talent', acting all the time so as to avoid getting three 'no's'. It is so easy to say 'yes' to those around us but if we are going to 'slay the dragon' we may have to be prepared to disappoint people. In many working environments today, there is an expectation that you will work harder and longer and be devoted to 'climbing the ladder' towards personal success. But what if when you reach the top rung you realise the ladder was up against the wrong wall all along? And all the time you have neglected the special people God has blessed you with - your family and friends.

I am all for working hard (see chapter 11). But work needs to form part of a healthy rhythm or balance to life - a rhythm that honours God. Sometimes an imbalance is driven by an insatiable desire to earn more and more money. Jesus tells a parable to address this topic about a rich fool who tore down his barns to build bigger ones in which to store his excess grain. That very night, his life was demanded of him and all his best laid plans lay in ruins.[35]

In John's gospel, we read of Jesus offering 'life in all its fullness.'[36] It is God's desire for our lives to be full (and fulfilled) not busy. A full life is one that is filled up with His plans and purposes. Nothing in this life can be as fulfilling or enriching as the plans and purposes that God

[35] Luke 12:13-21

[36] John 10:10

has for us. In just such a full life there will always be time to focus on the things that matter for eternity - and the God of all eternity. Busyness is the enemy of intimacy and God made us to be intimate with him and the friends and family He has given us.

Recently, I saw posted on Twitter, this memo from the then Vice President of the United States, Joe Biden. It inspires and encourages me so much that I offer it to you in full:

MEMORANDUM TO STAFF OF THE VICE PRESIDENT

FROM: VICE PRESIDENT BIDEN

RE: FAMILY OBLIGATIONS

DATE: NOVEMBER 7, 2014

To My Wonderful Staff,

I would like to take a moment and make something clear to everyone. I do not expect nor do I want any of you to miss or sacrifice important family obligations for work. Family obligations include but are not limited to family birthdays, anniversaries, weddings, any religious ceremonies such as first communions and bar mitzvahs, graduations, and times of need such as an illness or a loss in the family. This is very important to me. In fact, I will go so far as to say that if I find out that you are working with me while missing important family responsibilities, it will disappoint me greatly. This has been an unwritten rule since my days in the Senate.

Thank you all for the hard work,

Sincerely,

This is perhaps a principle that many, if not all of us would give our assent to. But being for a virtue and actually possessing it are two very different things. Sometimes we have to 'Just Say No'[37] to the myriad of requests on our time so that we can say 'yes' to our family and friends.

A classic piece of literature that I often find myself referring to is CS Lewis' The Screwtape Letters. It is a fictional piece of work where we, the readers get to hear an on-going dialogue between a senior and junior devil and in so doing we are able to imagine how their activity (and at times, in-activity) affects our lives here on earth. Given that so many of us lead such busy lives today, and as a result can, at times, find it difficult to be attentive to the voice of God, it seems to me that all the time I am busy, it may well be that the Enemy doesn't have to be. We end up distracting ourselves from the things we are meant to be doing with the people we really love.

At first sight, it would seem that New York Times bestselling author Kevin Kruse, and I would not have a great deal in common. It would appear that the motivation behind many or most of his tips and suggestions is to develop influence and make big money

---

[37] "Just Say No" was an advertising campaign, part of the U.S. "War on Drugs", prevalent during the 1980s and early 1990s, to discourage children from engaging in illegal recreational drug use by offering various ways of saying no. The slogan was created and championed by First Lady Nancy Reagan during her husband's presidency.

as a result.[38] But I love his books and what is more I find them full of useful and very practical hints for life that entirely translate for Christians wanting to live according to a rhythm of life that honours God. And so I am most grateful to Kruse for introducing me to 'the power of 1440'. "The single number that can change your life."[39]

1440 is the total number of minutes that every one of us has every single day. No-one can add to that number, no-one can steal some of it away. What each one of us must decide is how we are going to spend our 1440. Each of us must take responsibility for our own 1440, knowing that if we let people have '60 here or 30 there' then those are minutes we cannot spend devoted to people or tasks that are of the most importance to us. If you are someone who laments the number of interruptions you get each day, then he suggests putting a large poster with 1440 on it, on your office wall to remind you and those who may want "5 minutes of your time" that time is precious and how we spend it is so very important.

---

[38] My apologies if that is an unfair caricature.

[39] Kevin Kruse, *15 Secrets Successful People Know About Time Management*, Chapter 1

A simple prayer for the beginning of each day:

Dear Lord,

May my life be governed by God-given rhythms rather than the requirements and expectations of others.

Amen.

Suggestions

- PRIORITISE: Take some time out to identify who are the important people in your life and make sure your calendar reflects that level of importance.

- PLAN: Do not allow yourself to sleepwalk through a day, week or month. Time spent carefully planning your calendar is always well spent.

- PRACTICE: Be honest with yourself and hold yourself accountable. Do what you agreed you would do as represented in your calendar.

Questions

- Do you find it hard to say 'No' to people's requests? Can you identify why this is?

- Are you experiencing 'life in its fullness' or just a busy life?

- Do you have 'guilt-inducing' items on a 'to-do' list that have been there for longer than you care to remember?

7. Sabbath and Play

**Every seven days I will 'sabbath well',
meaning I will stop, rest, delight and
contemplate.**

The Sabbath was made for man, not man for the
Sabbath. So the Son of Man is Lord even of the Sabbath.
MARK 2:27-28

On Sabbath I embrace my limits. God is God. He is
indispensable. I am his creature. The world continues
working fine when I stop.
Peter Scazzero

I hope by now that you are beginning to recognise the importance of 'rhythm' within your life. A hugely important part of a good life rhythm is the concept of the Sabbath. By that I simply mean that one day in seven should look very different to the other six. In this chapter, I will attempt to explain what those differences look like for me.

Stop and think with me for a moment how rhythmical life itself is. How all created beings sleep - wake - repeat. How the brightness of Day gives way to the darkness of Night and then repeats. And then of course how, on an annual basis, the colour of Spring is followed by the heat of Summer, which gives way to the unpredictability of Autumn and then the cold of Winter[40]. And then it starts over again. Rhythm is good; it is an integral part of life; God made it that way.

Somehow, in society today, we seem to have adopted the ill-fated belief that good things only happen when you make them happen; when you work hard for them, chase them, or earn them. When we fail to get on board with God's intended rhythm of life, part of which is clearly to rest, we are in danger of missing some of the blessings that God wants to pour into our lives simply because He loves us and provides for us. All the time we labour and spin, we squeeze out God trying to prove that we are self-sufficient and His benevolence is superfluous.

---

[40] I recognise that I am writing from the UK and that in some parts of the world the seasons are less distinguishable.

Rest requires nothing of us - it should be effortless and yet nourishing. Without rest we adopt a survival mode and I am convinced that as His people, God wants us to thrive, not merely survive.[41]

A marker

At some point in reading this book you will presumably put a slip of paper or an equivalent at a certain point as a marker to help you remember where you are up to. A good Sabbath day acts as a marker to help you remember who you are, everything you have, and all the blessings God has poured into your life that past week and indeed over your life.

Looking back - Looking forward

Having said that, the Sabbath isn't just about looking back over the past week and reflecting upon it - as important as that is. The temptation is to think that the new week begins the day after the Sabbath and that as you work, you begin to count down the days until the Sabbath when you can rest again from your work. But in the Christian tradition, the Sabbath has always been on the first day of the week - Sunday (resurrection day) enabling you to work from your rest rather than rest from your work.[42] This is a subtle but important difference

---

[41] Again, John 10:10 springs to mind.

[42] Of course in the Jewish tradition of which Jesus was a part, Sabbath began at sundown on the Friday and went through until sundown on Saturday. That remains the case for Jews today.

because otherwise there is a danger that the Sabbath becomes just a 'day-off' on which you recover from the exertions of the working week. A true, life-enhancing Biblical Sabbath is much more than a day-off on which to run errands or engage in jobs around the house that need doing. Thankfully, many people (but I recognise not all) in the cultures of the Western world, still get a weekend off their paid work or two days together at some other time of the week. This enables something that resembles a day of preparation before Sabbath to get those necessary jobs done. Most people are weary in one form or another after 5/6 days work. A pre-Sabbath day (to give it a slightly awkward name) is the perfect antidote to that.

Work

Bear in mind that I am not saying that rest is good (and spiritual) and work is not. See chapter 11 as a counter to that way of thinking. What I am arguing is that we need both, and that the Sabbath acts as a balance point.

These same principles apply whether you are in paid employment or not. You may be retired, unemployed or a stay-at-home parent, the argument remains unchanged. I would say it is God's design that we rest one day a week from our regular work and on that day we approach life differently in order that God might refresh and renew us as part of our regular replenishment rhythm.

Before I lose readers who are parenting small (or indeed not-so-small) children or caring for elderly parents or vulnerable adults, allow me to add some 'grey' to my 'black and white' arguments.[43]

As a husband and father I have sympathy for any of you who are thinking, 'great in theory; what about the practice!' Packed lunches still have to be made, nappies changed, elderly parents cared for .....etc. etc.

But life does have its seasons and the reality is there will not always be people (young or old) who entirely depend on you. So recognise the season you are in and adjust your expectations accordingly. Sabbath can also be a state of mind. Sabbath periods, hours or moments, can be grabbed and God is there to be encountered right in the midst of your everyday activity.

Enslaved

When the People of God in the Old Testament ignored the 5th Commandment and failed to 'Remember the Sabbath day by keeping it holy' (Exodus 20:8) they were enslaving themselves all over again. Little has changed. Today, lifestyles are such that people consistently work seven days a week and then wonder why their health, key relationships and state of mind suffer and fail. God himself rested after six days of labour (Genesis 2:2), so

---

[43] We know that medical advancements mean that elderly parents are typically living longer and soaring house prices often mean that children remain in the parental home for longer as well.

why wouldn't I consider doing the same? There are four core elements to a Biblical Sabbath that I try to embrace.

Stop

As I do this, I am resisting the pull of the culture around me that urges me to work harder, longer, reach higher and generally strive for more. I am not defined by my work, output or achievements, rather I respond to a higher authority. Practically speaking, on my Sabbath I aim not to look at work-related text messages or emails and I never respond to them or phone calls. The truth of the matter is, people stop trying to contact you when they know you are not going to answer! Sabbath is humbling; it helps me deal with an exaggerated sense of self-importance.[44] It is also the perfect antidote to feeling guilty all day long for not doing something productive. (Of course, my whole argument is that Sabbath is incredibly productive but you know what I mean.) Some people need permission to stop - here is that permission!

However it is also worth acknowledging the very real fear that some people have on stopping. From the days of my youth, right up to this day, I have never been able to skim stones across a river or the sea. There is clearly something about my technique that is all wrong. What is sure is that a stone will only skim across water while it is travelling at pace. When it slows down, it sinks. Sometimes when we slow down, we sink too. And as we

---

[44] By that I mean the mis-guided belief that the world revolves around me!

sink, we discover something about ourselves that we didn't know before and perhaps didn't want to know. Sinking downwards is a chastening feeling. Better to keep the pace up - then we can keep going along nicely without ever having to face what is below the surface. Some people are afraid to stop in case they sink in the process. Take heart - as one who has sunk more often than he cares to remember, I know that God operates even more powerfully below the waterline than above it. [45]

Also, wisdom often comes to me when I stop on my Sabbath day. [46] It is remarkable how the simple act of stopping can bring clarity and vision. It is only when we stop our ceaseless doing that we really discover what needs to be done. [47]

Rest

This will look differently for different people but for me I catch up on sleep, I slow down (and infuriate other car drivers in the process) and I try not to clock-watch. As I do this, I am being a good steward of my body and soul. It's a day of no 'have-to's'.

---

[45] God's deepest work is done in our deepest, innermost places. Real character change that doesn't happen overnight.

[46] Along with a lot of crazy other ideas that my wife patiently listens to and watches pass by.

[47] This sounds like something I have heard John Ortberg say but I seem unable to attribute it to him. However he did coin the wonderful term "hurry sickness" in *The Life You've Always Wanted*.

Rest is an essential part of life, in fact think of it not unlike the very air you breathe. Without rest, we lack the energy we need to live life. It is not an optional extra, it is actually a non-negotiable.

Delight

Despite the plethora of entertainment options available to us today, many people are simply 'delight deficient'. And so, when I remember, I try to open my eyes and really take in the sights before me (escaping to the countryside or simply a park can help with this). On my sabbath, I like to eat good food and take time to actually taste it. I endeavour to do something for no other reason than I enjoy it and in so doing attempt to recapture some of that child-like delight which sadly we all lose. When we take time to walk in a forest or gaze at a view, or simply breathe deeply the fresh air, we do what we are told the Creator Himself did at the dawn of time:

God saw all that he had made, and it was very good.
GENESIS 1:31

It is hard to delight when you feel the lingering weight of worries and responsibilities. We need to offload them. Like airport-style security where phones, tablets, money and in fact all the contents of your pockets are emptied into a grey plastic box for whisking through the scanner, we need to give up those things that we habitually carry around with us for a while to enable us to truly delight in God and all the blessings he has bestowed upon us.

That delight may take the form of simply and deliberately remembering the truth of who you are in Christ that day rather than the person you feel you are invariably forced to be all week long.

Contemplate

In all of this I am trying to reflect on and sometimes reconnect with the love of God. This is not something you can hurry over; it takes time, it requires you to be with him. When I adjust my focus, I see everything more clearly and accurately. Sabbath is about earthing your sense of self in a relationship with God, not in your work or achievements. As this becomes part of our rhythm, as we increasingly make time to draw ever nearer to God, we find He is speaking (to us) all the time. I have lost count of the number of people I have met who say they never hear God speak. I myself have had extended periods where I have the sound of silence ringing in my ears. But so often that is because we are suffering with the disease of 'hurry', of which one of the symptoms is spiritual deafness. Our heads and hearts are so often filled with the noise of worries, busyness, drivenness or materialism that we are deaf to God's voice, His blessings, His call. His voice is drowned out and in my experience He rarely shouts. And because we fail to take time to be with Him and listen to that 'still small voice' we often end up acting before we know what to do, speaking before we know what to say and inadvertently making our complex lives even more complicated and confusing.

A note about prayer on the Sabbath. It maybe tempting to think that a Sabbath should be filled with prayers all day long but for me that often isn't the case. A simple prayer with a few words often does it for me. An acknowledgement that the day is a gift from God and a simple 'speak Lord for your servant is listening' type of prayer maybe all that is necessary at the outset of a Sabbath, before its delights are tasted.

Sabbath-time should form a key part of a God-honouring rhythm to your week, month and year. When my Dad taught me how to drive, he advised me never to let the fuel tank run down to empty because in so doing you would disturb all the nasty petrol residue from the tank and risk clogging up the carburettor. Best practice is to habitually refuel when the gauge reads 1/4 full. Taking a biblical weekly sabbath greatly reduces the risk of one's personal carburettor clogging up. It remains a gift from God and should be received as such. Do not wait for the gauge to read 'EMPTY' before stopping to refuel. Furthermore, Sabbath should infuse the rest of the week not be the response to the week that has passed. You should work out of rest, not rest from work.

The same principles apply to longer time periods. Time off and holidays need to be planned and then taken! In so doing, a regular sustainable rhythm is established so that you are more likely to thrive in life than merely survive it.

Suggestions

- Review your weekly, monthly, termly/quarterly and annual rhythm of life.

- If part of your work is to care for somebody else, talk with your spouse, a friend, a family member or support group member about how they can help you to sabbath?

- 'Empty your pockets' at the beginning of your Sabbath and resist the temptation to pick everything up again too soon.

Questions

- What collateral damage is there when you don't sabbath?

- What restores your soul? What gives you energy or revitalises you?

- What action do you need to take as a result of this chapter?

8. Generosity

I will consistently look for opportunities to be generous with my time, money and resources.

You will be enriched in every way so that you can be generous on every occasion.
2 CORINTHIANS 9:11

You have not lived today until you have done something for someone who can never repay you.
John Bunyan

Did I already mention that many of these principles have an aspirational element to them? Well that is most definitely the case with this one. I want to be a generous person, I know and understand the importance of being generous - it is just so very difficult! But I am committed to trying, which is why Generosity is in my Rule of Life.

There is a fundamental concept that lies at the heart of this topic that must be grasped: everything we have belongs to God and everything we are is down to Him.

This is so counter-cultural; it is so hard to move away from the thinking that asks 'how much of my money shall I give away.' It isn't just about money but typically that's where it hits us hardest. Everything we have comes from Him. Our question should rather be, 'What does God want me to do with the money/time/talents I have?'

Time

I have already dealt with the importance of good time management in chapter 6. If I am to 'consistently spend quality time with the people who are most important to me' then I am going to need to make every one of my 1440 minutes per day count. I should not be frittering them away. But the great danger of this mindset is that we become very selfish - very 'me' focused. This really is dangerous - it can do us great harm. I know that I run the risk of being so set on living my Rule of Life, that I fail to lift my head and see the genuine needs of those around me. In the West, we are typically 'cash rich and time poor'[48] so to give someone my time is more of a sacrifice than to give them some money. Many churches I know have a 'no money' policy when people come knocking on the door asking for help. This is entirely sensible as you never know what any money given will be spent on, but it really is inconvenient! When someone in need comes to the door, it means going with them to buy a sandwich or a travel card instead of sending them on their way with some cash to buy something themselves. And yet how much better it is to walk with them to the local store and talk as you go. In so doing you give them your money and your very precious time as well.

In the gospels we read that Jesus told a story about this in what we know as the Parable of the Good Samaritan.[49] There were probably a whole raft of reasons why the Priest and Levite rushed on by leaving the Samaritan man half-dead in the road. One was surely that neither of them wanted to make time to stop and help. Whatever they were doing, wherever they were on their way to, they thought it more important than the very real and obvious needs of the dying man. Time was of the essence and they were unprepared to give generously of theirs.

---

[48] For instance, by and large we would rather buy sandwiches from a convenience store at lunchtime than spend the time it takes to shop for the constituent parts and make the snack at home. Note, this is not a judgement, just a statement of fact for many.

[49] Luke 10:25-37

It is God who governs our comings and our goings and there are undoubtedly occasions when we find ourselves at just the right time and place to give generously of our time. Good, God-honouring plans sometimes need to be changed or shelved as we opt to be generous with our time.[50]

Money

I have been blessed to be on the receiving end of some amazing financial gifts over the years, from £20,000 for house redevelopment to money given for flights and accommodation for a major football tournament in France. Both were significant amounts of money given by generous people. Just as meaningful was the sum of £30 in cash pushed through our letterbox when times were hard with small children. Given anonymously but I am almost certain, sacrificially. I also used to meet a friend regularly for a cup of coffee who would get mildly annoyed if I didn't let him pay and allow him to exercise his gift of giving. The size of the gift is usually irrelevant - the heart with which it is given is the most significant thing. Some of the most generous people I know, earn a very modest salary.

I have long-held the view that a Christian's financial giving should begin with a commitment to the local church to which they belong. The Old Testament talks in terms of a 10% tithe but many people get hung up on

---

[50] See Mark 5:25-34 and Matthew 19:13-15 as two examples.

this and the New Testament is actually less specific. The relevant question maybe 'How can I use 10% as a guide to help me be generous?' Or to put it another way, 'How can I be generous in my financial giving and give back to God less than 10% of what He has given me?' Some people even lose sleep over tithing 'net or gross' but once again, surely this is missing the point. Generosity is about attitude of heart. A generous person does not ask 'what can I get away with giving / keeping?' but rather, 'How much can I give and can I give any more?'.

As part of my simple Rule of Life, I am trying to choose to live open-handedly. To fulfil my Christian obligation and then look to go over and above this by asking 'Who can I bless?', 'Where is there need?', 'How can I help?'. My wife helps me with this perspective.

Being generous with money is ultimately an issue of trust in God. If I choose to give away more of what God has given me, can I still trust Him to provide for all my needs? What I am learning is that being generous actually deepens my relationship with God as I learn to trust Him more and more. It is a double blessing! The recipient has their needs met and the giver makes a priceless investment in their on-going relationship with God.

Conversely, holding tightly to money and possessions merely serves to foster a self-reliance rather than a new-found 'God-reliance'. 'He can/will' is replaced with an 'I must' which brings with it all the associated anxieties of providing for ones own needs.[51]

Talents

Have you ever stopped to think about just how unique you are? There really is no-one in this world that is quite like you! Psalm 139 famously outlines that not only did God create us, but He knew us from our conception in intricate detail. Each one, completely unique - just as God intended.

One outworking of this is that each one of us therefore has a unique gift and talent mix. There are some things that you excel at and you thrive in doing them. It can be those very same things that I am hopeless at and have little interest in learning about. We should all be grateful for this because firstly, we need each other, and secondly, we all get to make a contribution.

In writing to the early church in Corinth, the Apostle Paul put it like this:

And so the body is not made up of one part but of many. Now if the foot should say, 'Because I am not a hand, I do not belong to the body,' it would not for that reason stop being part of the body. And if the ear should say, 'Because I am not an eye, I do not belong to the body,' it would not for that reason stop being part of the body. If the whole body were an eye, where would the sense of

---

[51] Let me make it clear that I am not against prudence or sound financial management. Both equate to good financial stewardship, which is to be applauded.

hearing be? If the whole body were an ear, where would the sense of smell be? But in fact God has placed the parts in the body, every one of them, just as he wanted them to be. If they were all one part, where would the body be? As it is, there are many parts, but one body.

1 CORINTHIANS 12:14-20

In the Body of Christ (the Church) we all have a role to play and each one has a set of gifts to bring. Singers, welcomers, speakers, musicians, coffee pourers, money counters, chair movers, Bible readers to name but a few. When we bring our gifts and talents, we create a beautiful thing together for the glory of God and the building of His kingdom.

We need to bring our gifts and talents generously in the service of others. What stops us? Sometimes we are lazy and just cannot be bothered. Other times we lack confidence and find it hard to believe that we can be of use in a church or other organisation. Sometimes the fear of failure paralyses us.

I'm sure I am not alone in noticing that a version of the Pareto Principle is commonly found in churches. Also known as the 80/20 Rule, the Pareto Principle states that for many events, roughly 80% of the effects come from 20% of the causes.[52] And so typically, 80% of the

---

[52] From https://en.m.wikipedia.org/wiki/Pareto_principle:
Management consultant Joseph M. Juran suggested the principle and named it after Italian economist Vilfredo Pareto, who noted the 80/20 connection while at the University of Lausanne in 1896.

necessary work in and around a church is done by 20% of its members. This really is not great. Not only is it grossly unfair on the 20% who are frantically busy and having real trouble living out chapter 6, but the 80% are missing out on the huge joy of identifying their unique God-given mix of gifts and the thrill of serving God and His people by using those gifts. We need to be generous with our talents and gifts.

Risk

Deciding to be generous with time, money and talents involves taking what might feel like a risk. More accurately it involves letting go and letting God be God.

In Matthew's gospel we read of an occasion when Jesus' disciples were out in a boat on the lake of Galilee, during the middle of the night. Suddenly, they see what looks like a ghost coming towards them, walking on the water. They soon realise that this is no ghost, it is Jesus and upon that realisation, Peter says to Jesus, 'If it's you, tell me come to you on the water.'[53] Then Peter does the most remarkable thing: he climbs out of the boat and begins to walk on the water towards Jesus.[54] Then we are told that he sees the wind, becomes afraid and begins to sink. The inference is that he takes his eyes off Jesus. Peter took a risk, made a literal step of faith and had a

---

[53] Matthew 14:28

[54] This was no stream - the Sea of Galilee is 43 metres at its deepest point.

life-changing experience as a result. Arguably, he trusted Jesus like no-one had ever done before.

Being generous with our time, money and talents can feel like taking a risk or making a new step of faith. In doing so, the key for us (as with Peter) is to keep our eyes on Jesus; to put our trust in Him. He will not let us fall or let the waves engulf us. It truly is only when we loosen the grip on all that we possess, that our hand is free to grab hold of His, which is a far better place for it to be.

Suggestions

- Schedule one hour a week to do something for someone who can never repay you.

- Work out what 10% of your annual income is and then compare that figure to what you currently give away.

- Identify your unique mix of gifts and give consideration as to how you might best serve the community you belong to. Note: talking this through with someone who knows you and who you can trust, can often be helpful.

Questions

- What is stopping you from being radically generous?

- Do you find it most difficult to be generous with your time, your money or your talents?

- What can you do now on the road to a newly-found level of generosity?

9. Study and Learning

Given that God is so big and I am so small, I will take every opportunity to learn something new about Him and His world.

Get wisdom, get understanding; do not forget my words or turn away from them.

PROVERBS 4:5

You are never too old to set another goal or to dream a new dream.

CS Lewis

I came to faith in a fast-growing evangelical church in St Neots near Cambridge. As a young person, it was a great place to be as there was always plenty going on and the youth group was large and vibrant. I am forever indebted to my church leaders of that time who gave me such a solid Biblical foundation of belief that has formed the basis of my ministry for over 20 years now.

In 1993, I went to London Bible College (now London School of Theology) which at the time was Europe's largest independent theological training centre. It truly was a life-changing experience. As I reflect on that time now, I recognise that broadly speaking during my three-year course, year one was spent dismantling my 'neat and tidy' faith, in year two we explored deeply matters of theology and the Christian faith, and then in year three my faith was put back together again. I am so grateful for this experience because I know now that God is so much bigger than one church or domination recognises. Before college, my faith was sincere but narrow.

Thus I began the process of continually discovering the wonder of God; how beautiful and at the same time complex He is. Although this is when I began that process in earnest,[55] it is one that has undoubtedly continued ever since - and indeed will continue until my dying day. In terms of understanding, knowing and experiencing God, I / we are only just getting started.

---

[55] Of course, the process really began the moment I first became aware of the existence of God.

God is big!

How many of you are able to identify with that feeling of dread that comes over us when an 'action song' is announced at church? You can just about cope with flinging your arms around or running on the spot when you have young children with you because you can see the greater good. But as soon as they reach the age where the last thing they want to see is Dad making a fool of himself, the whole thing becomes awkward and uncomfortable. And yet, some of those songs are rich in theological truth and we would do well to take their message to heart. Take for instance, Great Big God.[56] One of the reasons why that song has become so universally popular is because it teaches an absolutely fundamental truth about God in a way that a person of just about any age can understand. And yet, many of us live our lives in a way that keeps God contained in a neat and tidy, manageable box. Surely God cannot and should not be managed.

A commitment to Study and Learning guards against this and underscores the truth that God is vast, mysterious and ultimately beyond our comprehension. And I for one would not have it any other way. I do not want my God to be fully explainable.

Similarly, a commitment to Study and Learning reaffirms a desire to be a true follower of Christ. By living out a

[56] *Great Big God* - written by Nigel and Jo Hemming, Vineyard Records, 2001

simple Rule of Life and by constantly learning as part of that, we remain open to the Spirit of God changing us, re-shaping us and ultimately making us more like Christ.

This requires humility and a willingness to hold up one's hands and say "I do not know!". This is not entirely popular today as increasingly we live in an age of advancement and understanding.

To not be able to explain the activity of God may prove unsatisfactory for some but at the same time it is refreshingly liberating. Not everything or everyone can be known or understood and that certainly goes for God. There is always more to learn and discover about Him.

Books

Clearly there are a number of ways we can increase our learning; reading books is definitely one of mine. It seems I am not alone - despite the emergence of the e-book that has changed the way we read markedly, reports in 2015 suggest that good old-fashioned paper and ink is experiencing somewhat of a resurgence in popularity.[57] I use both which is why I rarely walk past an Oxfam Bookshop without popping in to check the Religion section. Part of the reason why I do that is because there may always be the opportunity to pick up something a little different or a title that doesn't sit on my current 'wish-list'. This way, my horizons are widened and

[57] http://www.telegraph.co.uk/culture/books/booknews/11335718/The-Kindle-is-dead-the-book-is-back.-Or-is-it.html

I am more open to God speaking to me about Himself and His world.

We live in an age when almost any book title, past or present, can be delivered to your door - many the very next day. So be inquisitive about what other people are reading and try not to limit yourself to safe and familiar titles that will merely reinforce your established view of God.

I once read of a political strategist who at a New Year's Eve party in 2005 challenged the then President of the US, George W. Bush to a competition to see who could read the most books in the coming year. Bush was narrowly defeated 110 books to 95.[58] What I find absolutely remarkable is that the 'Leader of the free world' made time to read 95 books in one year! Even though he had reached the pinnacle of his working life, clearly Bush still maintained a desire to carry on studying and learning.

People (Mentoring)

As well as reading books (to which you can add blogs and other online posts) I recognise that I learn a great deal from spending time with great people - some formally, much of it informally. A willingness to learn from other people requires an openness, a humility and a vulnerability that does not come naturally to many of us. I

---

[58] Read in *15 Secrets Successful People Know About Time Management* by Kevin Kruse

have four or five 'mentors' who speak into the various aspects of my life, not all of whom would recognise themselves as such.

Typically a mentor will be someone you trust and know who holds a degree of expertise in a given area. There is no set way that the mentoring relationship has to work - it is a case of finding out what works best for you. Some of the key people who have spoken into my life over the years I would take out for coffee or lunch periodically to glean their wisdom. There is one who I have for over 10 years taken a 100+ mile round trip to spend a couple of hours with twice a year. Another is an elderly retired pastor who lives in the US and we have exchanged letters for over 20 years. In the age of technological advancement, I experience the joys of FaceTime or Skype with another. Then on top of this, there are ones I have never personally met! Leaders from around the world 'mentor me' in the area of Christian Leadership through reading their books/articles, listening to their podcasts and watching their talks online.

A mentor would typically be more experienced than you in your given area (although not necessarily older in years) and willing to give up their time with the agreed frequency. You will have to make the running - initiate the meetings, undertake the travelling, buy the coffee, etc. Similar to a mentor, but with a slightly different agenda or approach, is the grandiosely titled Spiritual Director who can help you discern God's activity in your life and His plans and purposes for you going forward.

Whether they are mentors, spiritual directors or just good friends, people are invaluable in helping us learn more about God and His world.

Places

I wonder, do you deliberately go to places where you know you will learn something new? For the past ten years or so, my family and I have made the long late July trip to Shepton Mallet for the New Wine Summer Festival[59]. A good time is generally had by all (as long as it is not raining) and as a family we have enjoyed going immensely. Personally, I benefit because some of what I see and hear challenges me greatly. It forces me to reflect on the nature of God and His activity in the world today. I do not always agree with everything I hear, which I believe is all the more reason to go! Secretly, we all think we hold a sound and balanced theology - New Wine helps me to keep mine balanced.

For the past decade, I have also maintained a regular commitment to attend the Annual Global Leadership Summit[60] as it is streamed in locations across the UK. So vast is the amount of material you gain exposure to here that the real trick is to make time after the event to revisit it and inwardly digest. Every time I attend, I learn a huge amount about Christian Leadership and in so doing I know I am living out part of my own simple Rule of Life.

---

[59] See www.new-wine.org

[60] See www.willowcreek.org.uk

When I read a broad range of books, articles and posts, spend time with wise people and visit places outside my comfort zone, my ever-shrinking Christian worldview is expanded and that helps me to keep learning. I have the tendency to 'play it safe' and therefore limit God by reducing Him to a controllable 'father-figure' who I can call on when it suits me.

Remember, the truth you gain from within your own circle of comfort will only ever be partial because our circles tend to be pretty small. If everyone is made in the image of God (as Genesis 1:27 tells us) then surely we can learn something about God from everyone, even if at times His nature is imperfectly reflected.

Suggestions

- Never walk past an Oxfam bookshop without popping in.

- Companies like Amazon have a 'Wishlist' facility online to which you can add titles you hear people talk about or recommend.

- Be gracious enough to 'hear someone out' even if you disagree with some of what they are saying.

Questions

- What are you currently reading? Will it expand your vision and understanding of God?

- When was the last time you visited a place of worship that you knew would challenge your understanding of God?

- How might you go about measuring your own growth in your understanding of God?

10. Speaking Up

I will not stay silent when words of truth, hope or love need to be said.

Speaking the truth in love, we will grow to become in every respect the mature body of him who is the head, that is, Christ.

EPHESIANS 4:15

If he has faith, the believer cannot be restrained.
He betrays himself. He breaks out. He confesses and teaches this gospel to the people at the risk of life itself.

Martin Luther

So there I am, stuck in the middle of Lisbon. On holiday with my family, we are booked on a tour of the city due to commence in half an hour and we cannot get a bus or tram to where we need to be. The answer to our problem arrives in the form of a Tuk Tuk that will take us to where we're going. "I'll take you right by your tour bus", promises the driver, so we hop on and begin to enjoy the ride. Except it soon becomes obvious that he doesn't know exactly where we need to be - he's checking his phone for directions as we hurtle along. Twenty minutes later, we pull up and our 'ever-so-pleasant' Tuk Tuk driver claims we have arrived. We look around and nobody else is there, no queue of expectant sightseers is forming, there's no tour bus in sight. We disembark, I hand over the agreed €20 and off he speeds quicker than you can say Tchau.[61] Why didn't I say something? Why didn't I question whether this was really it? Why didn't I politely ask the driver to do what he promised he would do for us? Why did I lead my family into a ten minute mad-dash along the dockside to the real pick-up point, rendering us breathless and frustrated?[62] Why didn't I speak up?

Adam and Eve

When the woman saw that the fruit of the tree was good
for food and pleasing to the eye, and also desirable for
gaining wisdom, she took some and ate it. She also gave

---

[61] The Portuguese for 'goodbye' in case you were wondering.

[62] The story has a happy ending. We made it in time (just) and the tour was one of the highlights of the holiday.

some to her husband, who was with her, and he ate it.

The first Biblical example of someone not speaking up when they should have done may have come about just three chapters in. In Genesis chapter 3 we read that the serpent tricks or tempts Eve into believing that eating the fruit from the tree in the middle of the garden would not be as disastrous as God had in fact suggested. But we read in 3:6 that having eaten the fruit herself, Eve gives some to Adam who was with her. If Adam was with or alongside her all along, then he heard the conversation she had with the serpent, he witnessed the deception, he assessed the situation and then chose to remain silent. What a catastrophic error of judgement.[63] Sometimes staying silent really does carry with it a huge price-tag.

I have decided I don't want to be the sort of person who is overwhelmed or intimidated by situations or people and therefore unable to speak up for truth, justice or what I believe in. I don't want to be afraid to share my perspective because sometimes, when I stay silent, it feels like a little piece of me dies inside. I am disappointed, depressed and frustrated, all at the same time. Each one of us is faced with a choice in such circumstances. Do we risk being rebuffed or rejected? Or do we remain silent and risk not being true to ourselves? I want to be an individual who speaks his mind and is not

[63] Admittedly, the apostle Paul is happy to lay the blame squarely at the feet of Eve in 1 Timothy 2:13-14 but Genesis 3:6 does say he was *with* her.

afraid to share his thoughts. Having some things that are important to me, is in itself, important to me! Just as crucial is having the courage to talk about such things openly and honestly. Understand that I don't want to come across as arrogant but neither do I want to be so worried about what people think of me that I 'clam-up' and am not able to express myself.

Does not wisdom call out?
Does not understanding raise her voice?
PROVERBS 8:1

This verse from Proverbs gives us permission to speak up and speak out - to find our voice. If you have got something to say, then say it! Don't bottle it up or push it down.

Silence

The phrase 'Silence is golden' implies that refraining from speech is at times an option to be favoured and indeed it is. But this is actually part of a less often used saying, 'Speech is silver, silence is golden.' There is nothing wrong with speaking! But clearly there is a time and a place, as the book of Ecclesiastes recognises there is 'a time to remain silent, and a time to speak.' (Ecclesiastes 3:7)

Sometimes it is absolutely right to say nothing. You may feel the need or urge to speak out but realise at the same time that your motives may not be pure or good. Our motives for acting or speaking are invariably mixed anyway so a good look at your heart is always a good thing.

So when you feel the need to speak up, examine your own life. What is your reason for saying this? Is it a pride issue? Is your aim simply to convince the other party of your perspective or viewpoint? To, as it were, win the argument? Or rather, are you seeking to broaden their understanding and bring additional perspective which allows them to make a more informed decision? This is particularly pertinent when speaking to those who hold some sort of authority over you. You will gain the respect of your bosses if you respectfully challenge them, offering a different viewpoint, whilst at the same time acknowledging that they are the boss and the final decision is likely to be theirs. Asking questions is not the same as questioning and it is always possible to disagree with someone whilst remaining positive, supportive and respectful.

God gave us two ears and only one mouth for a reason and ears are not just for resting glasses on! As James 1:19 puts it, 'My dear brothers and sisters, take note of this: everyone should be quick to listen, slow to speak and slow to become angry.' When having a conversation, listening is never optional! What we do have a choice over is whether to speak or stay silent. Lord, give me wisdom to know which to do! Sometimes there is no choice - you have to speak out. Matters of injustice cannot be ignored, mistreatment, abuse or inequality cannot go unchallenged. Martin Luther King Jr. famously said, 'In the end, we will remember not the words of our enemies but the silence of our friends.'

When we face untenable or upsetting situations we cannot simply pretend we didn't see or hear them. We have to speak out otherwise the angst gets pushed down inside, buried deep within and causes further grief or frustration.

In church meetings I try to make it an understood rule that opinions are always welcomed when they are shared respectfully. Silence in such a meeting can lead to murmuring, discontent and gossiping out of it. People who do not speak up in a meeting but then share their thoughts with a select few afterwards, threaten to undermine the group and its leader. 'Car park conversations' are unhealthy and divisive.

Speaking up about Jesus

I write this chapter on the Feast Day of St Francis of Assisi. As well as being remembered as a gentle and generous man whose life was radically altered in response to God, Francis is attributed as saying, "Preach the gospel by all means and if necessary use words."[64]

Our very lives ought to be a living example of the message our mouths carry. Our words and our actions should complement each other, not convey mixed

---

[64] Whether or not he actually said this is debated but the sentiment would have been his.

messages. For some, these words attributed to St Francis provide an excuse for not speaking of Jesus or proclaiming the gospel. But 1 Peter 3:15 leaves us no doubt in this matter.

Always be prepared to give an answer to everyone who asks you to give the reason for the hope that you have.[65]

Many people (myself included) find it very hard to talk to people about the person of Jesus Christ and the way He transforms lives. All the more reason for me to include 'Speaking Up' in my Rule of Life and for you to consider doing the same. It's impossible for me to under-estimate my own propensity towards self-protection, selfishness or self-preservation. This is why I need the Holy Spirit to constantly deal with me in these areas.

All of this links back into the wider task we are engaged in as we develop a personal Rule of Life. In so doing, we are really asking God to highlight for us those things that are of most importance. What is important per se? What is God pinpointing for me? What may be of importance (to God) but is for someone else to pick up and run with? If we prayerfully and carefully engage in this process, we will more likely know what we simply have to speak up about and what we can or indeed should remain silent over.

In all of this, be kind to yourself - don't beat yourself up.

---

[65] Read on and you'll see that the verse urges that this be done with gentleness and respect.

Mistakes and missed opportunities are part of life and are helpful if we learn from them. You cannot go through life full of regret, wishing you'd said something or intervened on certain occasions. That said, I'm learning that although speaking up can be incredibly hard, the alternative can be truly devastating.

Common reasons for not speaking up to think about:

- You feel no one will listen.

- You feel intimidated by the environment and/or the people you're with and so feel uncomfortable expressing your views or opinions.

- You may be fearful of the repercussions.

- You hate conflict, confrontation or find it difficult to make hard decisions.

- You care too much what people think!

Suggestions

- Pray before a potentially difficult conversation.

- Listen well, choose your words carefully and show respect to a person with whom you disagree.

- Remember the goal should always be to add understanding to a situation and where appropriate express opinions. Don't set out to prove a point or even 'win'.

- Repent and ask for forgiveness if you've spoken out of turn or used the wrong tone. Recognise there's always the possibility you may be wrong!

Questions

- Consider for a moment whether you are more likely to speak up when you should stay silent or vice versa?

- Do you care too much what people think about you? Ask God to help you let go of this.

- What is the most difficult part for you about speaking about Jesus?

- Have you identified your 'non-negotiable' issues that you cannot stay silent over?

11. Working Diligently

I will work hard and smart within the reasonable time allotted to do so.

Whatever you do, work at it with all your heart,
as working for the Lord.
COLOSSIANS 3:23

Pray as though everything depended on God.
Work as though everything depended on you.
Augustine

This morning I woke up with a song in my head - The Boomtown Rats classic 1979 UK Number One, 'I Don't Like Mondays'. The song was penned by Bob Geldolf in the aftermath of a shooting by a 16-year-old girl at Grover Cleveland Elementary School in San Diego, California, on 29 January 1979. Two adults were killed, and eight children and one police officer were injured. The young girl's explanation for her actions went along the lines of her not liking Mondays.

The song was most likely in my head because this week I am back at work after a great two-week vacation. That said, I love my job and I really wasn't dreading going back to work at all.

But the way some people talk about their work makes your heart sink. How they spend all week counting down the days until the weekend and then spend the weekend dreading Monday mornings. Many clock watch when they are there and can't wait to be out of the door when home time comes. Now I am fortunate in that my job comes with a fair amount of flexibility. I can often make it to a school assembly or break off for a game of squash in the day (see chapter 7: Sabbath and Play). But it's not all peace and joy! Remember, when many are winding down at 5pm on a Friday, as a Priest, my mind is beginning to 'crank-up' as I begin to get ready for my busiest period of the week. I remember being called up at 6pm one Saturday to go to the local hospital and pray for a stranger whose life end was imminent. What an utter privilege and at the same time, such hard work!

I have included this principle in my Rule of Life because of what I believe about work - specifically my Theology of Work.

What makes work ultimately life-giving and rewarding is the attitude we have towards it. If it is negative and gloomy and we are determined to be bored then that is exactly what we will be. If we follow Paul's exhortation to 'work as if working for the Lord'[66] then a joy that comes from knowing God's pleasure really can be found in stacking beer cans in your local supermarket. (Believe me, it's a real challenge to think that perfectly aligning beer cans at 2am in the morning is honouring God but personal experience confirms to me that it can be done!) Similarly, changing a nappy for the nth time in a day can be somewhat of a drain (let's be honest!) and yet at the same time fulfilling and hugely rewarding.

Work is God's gift to us. (You may need to read that sentence again!) And if God gives you a gift then it must be good.[67]

If one of the reasons you are looking forward to heaven is the chance to put your feet up, you may have to think again. In the book of Genesis we read that work pre-existed the Fall.[68] It seemed good to God to have

---

[66] Colossians 3:23

[67] If you have any doubt about this then read Matthew 7:9-11

[68] Genesis 2:15 The Lord took the man and put him in the Garden of Eden to work it and take care of it.

humankind working the land so that it would yield what was needed for sustenance. It was only after Adam and Eve's bad decision-making that this work became hard and wearisome.[69]

Where do we go to in order to catch an imperfect glimpse of what the New Heaven and the New Earth will look like? Well Revelation yes, but also Genesis 1-2 - the perfect world that God created first time round, spoiled by human hands. My very real sense is that we will have work to do in heaven and that it will be the most rewarding work ever! We will love it and find it so fulfilling.

By dropping the 'work is bad' rhetoric we can begin to embrace our labour as the gift God intends it to be. That being the case, our attitude towards it can and should be to work diligently - doing the best we possibly can and in so doing honouring God and finding fulfilment.

Maybe you've gone through a period of unemployment or been close to someone who has? How devastating that can be! This is because we are made to work, to contribute to the well-being of society; to gain a sense of achievement and satisfaction. Unemployment robs you of these things and can send people into a downward spiral of depression. During such periods, you may question whether there's anything worth getting out of bed for in the morning.

---

[69] Genesis 3:17-19

Of course, work isn't only the activity that one gets paid for. All of us have work to do, all of the time. Whether you're a stay-at-home parent, a student at school or college, or you've retired from paid work, everyone has work to do that can be done to the glory of God.

Meanwhile, there is much talk today of getting a good 'work-life' balance. I personally dislike the phrase because it perpetuates a compartmentalising of our life that God would have us see as a whole. It implies that work is what we get over or through in order to start living, whereas work is very much part of life.[70] What's more it perpetuates the false 'sacred-secular' divide, claiming some activities are spiritual and others not so. Everything is spiritual - nothing is beyond the realm and rule of God. All of it will disappear when He decides it is time. This is what makes Colossians 3:23 so important. Every activity you are engaged in can be done with and for the glory of God.[71] And it is His intention that we find joy and fulfilment in all we do, whether in 'work, rest or play'.[72]

That said, it is worth stating that working diligently does not necessarily mean working longer. So many people

---

[70] Research suggests the average person will spend a third of their life at work or 57% of their waking time during a 45 year working life.

[71] This has significant implications for how we might 'Play Hard' as well.

[72] Older readers will know that I have shamelessly stolen this phrase from the Mars Bar adverts of the 70's and 80's. A Mars a day helps you work, rest and play. Dentists weren't as convinced.

today have to work long hours and the expectations placed upon them seem inescapable. I am both sympathetic to this predicament but also a pragmatist. I know people who every time I meet them will say, "work is just a bit busy at the moment" or "I'm in a busy season at work." For some, that season seems to have lasted a decade or more and their children have grown up in the meantime. We should not fool ourselves. Seasons have a start point and an end point - and they change. As I write, the temperature outside is below freezing and we are in the grip of winter. But in just a few short weeks, I know Spring will be upon us.

Working diligently for me involves working hard, applying effort, honouring God, and increasingly, working smarter. To that end I have begun to take an interest in trying to implement little tricks or subtle changes in behaviour that result in an increase in my productivity and a better use of my time. There is a whole raft of material available on this, much of which focuses on how through increased productivity you can become more or even massively wealthy. That doesn't interest me and is not my motivation but I believe many of the principles do translate for someone seeking to live as a Disciple of Christ and at the same time, work hard. Here are a few of the tips I have picked up that help me in my quest to Work Diligently:

- I am responsible for my use of time, of which everyone has exactly the same amount - 1440 minutes a day to be precise.

- I have abandoned 'To-Do' lists - they enslave you and rob you of the joy of having had a really productive day.[73] If something is important enough to be done, it makes it straight onto my calendar.

- My calendar reflects my values. This is essentially what Rule of Life is all about. Do what is important to you (and God) and don't spend time on what is not.

- I am prepared to disappoint people! Now understand that I don't deliberately set out to do this but if you are focused on achieving what is most important to you and God, you will inevitably disappoint people around you whose priorities are different. Be a people-pleaser and you will miss your goals, your output may fall and most likely you'll disappoint others anyway!

- I do not confuse working diligently with having to be perfect. Remember, there will always be more to do than can realistically be done.

- I do not allow my sense of self-worth to get tied up with what I do or produce. Each one of us is valuable and precious to God because of who we are, not because of what we do.

At the end of a long day, I can lay my head on the pillow, perhaps physically and mentally exhausted, but satisfied

---

[73] Many of us never complete a 'to-do' list and consequently they exist as a constant reminder of things left undone or outstanding.

in knowing I have worked diligently in the tasks that God has given me to do. Tomorrow it will start all over again but that is not for now.[74] Now is for rest and contentment.

Is there such a thing as 'working Christianly'? Swiss theologian, Emil Brunner wrote, "The Christian community has a specific task. . . . to regain the lost sense of work as a divine calling."[75] If we see the work set before us as not only given to us by God but also a daily opportunity to glorify Him through our diligence and application, then surely our attitude to that work will be transformed - for the better. And God can and will equip us for our 'good work'. The prayer at the end of the letter to the Hebrews[76], need not only apply to what might broadly be seen as 'Christian work'. We all need to see work in a slightly broader context.

As I seek to Work Diligently, I am inspired by the example of St Alphonsus Rodriguez. Born in 1532 in Segovia, Spain, Rodriguez sensed a call and vocation to religious life and applied to join the Jesuit Order. But he found his application refused because he had struggled in his schooling and was relatively uneducated. But he was finally accepted as a lay brother in 1571 and was sent to Montesione College on the island of Majorca where, remarkably, he served as a doorkeeper for 45 years. This

---

[74] Matthew 6:34

[75] Emil Brunner, cited by Mark Greene, *Thank God It's Monday.*

[76] Hebrews 13:20-21

job enabled him to minister to many visitors and he became spiritual advisor to numerous students. How do you operate joyfully as a doorkeeper for 45 years? Surely by recognising your work as being a service to God and an opportunity to glorify Him through doing simple tasks faithfully and diligently.

Suggestions

- Block out time in your calendar each day to accomplish tasks that need to be done. Treat them like dentist appointments that you wouldn't ignore!

- Put a big 1440 sign on your office wall to remind you (and others) just how many minutes there are in each day.

- Consider using a polite 'Please Do Not Disturb' sign on your door when you are engaged in an activity that requires your undivided attention.

- Pray before, during and about your work and see the difference it makes!

Questions

- Are you happy in your work? If not, what can be done?

- Who would you say you are working for?

- Do you have a 'Theology of Work'?

- Could the detail of this chapter help you maximise your 1440?

12. Theological Reflection

I will reflect theologically on the joyful and painful realities of everyday life, endeavouring to see God at work in the world.

'For my thoughts are not your thoughts, neither are your ways my ways,' declares the LORD. 'As the heavens are higher than the earth, so are my ways higher than your ways and my thoughts than your thoughts.'

ISAIAH 55:8

Suffering is unbearable if you aren't certain that God is for you and with you.

Tim Keller

The final component of my Rule of Life suggests that we reflect on life in all its complexity through a theological lens. You may have picked up by now that I believe it is vitally important that having faith in Christ impacts every single part of life. Every decision, every day, should be influenced by the reality of faith. That includes the mountain-top highs and the valley-like lows.

This chapter is basically an attempt to be honest - to myself, with God and to the world around me. In practice, what that means is I am not going to shy away from the difficulties one faces when you integrate life and faith together. My desire is to acknowledge the struggles and face them, whilst at the same time maintaining a firm grip on a God who is good on every day and in every way.

As followers of Jesus we know we are in the presence of God all of the time and His Spirit lives within us.[77] God is active in the world all the time; He is not distant or apart from it. In all its complexity, He is in the midst of life. This principle is about acknowledging that and learning to see God in the world and discern His activity. It won't always lead to absolute understanding as to what God is doing - we have already established that He is not entirely knowable and remains ultimately beyond our comprehension. But when we learn to see Him at work, what results is a peace that is ours regardless of the circumstances in which we find ourselves. It is a peace that the world cannot give.

---

[77] Romans 8:9

Peace I leave with you; my peace I give you. I do not give to you as the world gives. Do not let your hearts be troubled and do not be afraid.

JOHN 14:27

If this principle is to be a reality in our life then one of the first lessons to learn is that sometimes (maybe even often in my experience!) God's activity in the world often looks suspiciously like inactivity to us. They say that hindsight is a wonderful thing. Well how many times have you looked back on your life and been able to see that God was working His purposes out all along? Some times you may even breathe a sigh of relief that God did not in fact answer your prayers in quite the way you wanted.

It is easy to say, I know, but it is precisely during these times that we would do well to reflect theologically on our life and the world. And it is during these times that our prayers become real, honest and heartfelt: God what are you doing? Why are you not doing this for me? Where are you? Why can I not hear you, see you, feel you? At these times our cry to God echoes that of the Psalmist. [78]

And whilst genuinely feeling the pain, anguish or doubt that is within us, refusing to ignore or suppress it, we can hold on to the truth of this wonderful promise:

---

[78] Often called 'Psalms of lament' examples include Psalm 44, 60 and 74.

And we know that in all things God works for the good of
those who love him, who have been called
according to his purpose.

ROMANS 8:28

There is great comfort and hope for us in this verse but it is worth acknowledging that it is often mis-quoted or mis-understood. It does not mean that God wills everything to happen or is the architect of the difficult situations we face. What it does tell us is that even in the most desperate circumstances, He works for good and will bring good outcomes to bear. Often we feel sad, confused or overwhelmed by life's ups and downs. Our emotions are tossed back and forth by events happening close to home, influencing family, friends or colleagues and those far away beamed into our homes via television, computer or mobile phone. Voices in the world shout loudly at us everywhere we turn and we cannot make sense of it or we simply cannot cope. Thank God there is a God! This is the time to cling to Him and to ask Him to help us see things like He does. To learn to think, to feel and indeed to perceive theologically.

What is undeniable is that sooner or later in life, we will be confronted with situations that raise questions about meaning, purpose and the value of our life. We or a loved one falls ill. Redundancy strikes. Exam results are disappointing. Somebody lets us down. And at these times, we wouldn't be human if we did not question the role of God in these situations and others in the world at large.

As I write, an earthquake has just struck off the coast of Japan triggering a tsunami alert, a train has crashed in India killing 140 people and injuring many more, and yet another friend has broken news of a cancer diagnosis.

We need to reflect theologically on these and indeed all of life's events. In prayer we need to search for God in them - for He is to be found. God is never absent in life's ups and downs. He never takes a break, books time off or switches off for a while.

Genuine theological reflection starts with important questions like 'God where are you?' 'What are you doing in this situation?' Even 'Why God?' Such questions promote open, honest prayer before God and they nurture maturity in faith; they help us to grow up. On one level it might seem somewhat immature to, as it were, have a tantrum in front of God like a small child does who doesn't get their way. But in reality, complete honesty with God in prayer is what He desires and our willingness to hold nothing back demonstrates that we have understood this and indeed what prayer itself really is.

In practising this principle, I am saying I will not settle for trite answers offered to life's big questions. I can never pretend to have all the answers but I will never give up in my pursuit of the One who knows the beginning from the end. The One who is indeed the Alpha and Omega.[79]

---

[79] Revelation 21:6

In terms of witness, the last thing the world needs is Christians putting on happy smiling faces and pretending everything is okay when clearly it is not. At times, 'Life sucks', but at those times I am not alone and God is neither absent or impotent.

Christians need to bring a mature perspective into the pain and the suffering that at times seems so prevalent. A perspective that has God in it changes everything.

In Genesis 32:22-32 we read the account of Jacob wrestling with God at Peniel all night long until He gives him a blessing. What a powerful image that is. The pursuit of God through relentless and indeed strenuous theological reflection helps us discern what He is doing in the world and (importantly) in our own lives specifically. Once we begin to understand even a small part of that, we surely also begin to evaluate and assess life's events from a more rounded, more godly, perspective.

Dutch Catholic priest and theologian Henri Nouwen defines Theological Reflection as "reflecting on the painful and joyful realities of every day with the mind of Jesus and thereby raising human consciousness to the knowledge of God's gentle guidance."[80]

How I need my human consciousness raised! As you read this, perhaps your reflection might be the same. The

---

[80] Henri J Nouwen, *In the Name of Jesus*, p68

more we can operate with the 'mind of Christ'[81] the better the little part of the world that we inhabit will be. And in us, something deeply spiritual will be formed.

I recently attended the funeral of a friend whose life was cut tragically short. The service was beautifully and sensitively led, her family spoke movingly and passionately about her life and as a congregation we proclaimed God's goodness using her favourite songs and hymns. As we drove home, my wife and I reflected on why we were feeling as we were and what it was that was missing from the service. Then it came to me, there was little or no space to publicly voice the injustice of the situation. To say out loud how unfair it all was and how angry we were with disease, death, even with God! A time for such reflection would have been awkward and messy but ever so healing. Part of my theological reflection on the long car journey home that day was that God was himself angry with disease and death as well. And in that reflection, I found comfort....

---

[81] 1 Corinthians 2:16

Suggestions

- Ask God to show you how and where He is present in the world's most difficult situations right now.

- Take some time to reflect on one or two of life's difficult situations and see if, in retrospect, you can sense the activity of God.

- If you are struggling to experience the reality of God in your current difficulties, ask a trusted friend to pray with you that God would make Himself known.

Questions

- Are you able to 'rant' before God concerning injustice or pain?

- Could a regular reading of the Psalms help you be more honest with God in prayer?

- What action do you need to take as a result of reading about this final principle? For instance, find someone you can trust who can help you see God working through your difficulties.

Over to You

Writing your own Rule of Life

When I created the Rule of Life group towards the end of 2015, we began to meet twice a month - once for teaching and input and once to eat, socialise and reflect together. The second of these monthly meetings took place at various local restaurants which provided the perfect setting for the conversation to flow. On one occasion, we met outside the agreed Greek restaurant only to find it closed, so we needed to decamp somewhere else. I had spotted a new Italian restaurant that had just opened up around the corner and I suggested we give it a try. Paolo (our Italian group member) disappeared to check it out only to return shaking his head. He explained that they did not have a wood-fired oven so it really was not an authentic Italian restaurant. He explained that real pizza has to be cooked in a wood-fired oven, which gets extremely hot. Therefore real authentic pizza should only be cooked for 3-4 minutes - at a very high temperature.

Now you and I know that pizza comes in all shapes and sizes. You have the 'cheap' supermarket versions and those you can pick up from the American inspired takeaway outlets. But according to Paolo, until you have tasted a Neapolitan wood-fired pizza, you really haven't tasted pizza at all. If you come from Naples, the others may look like pizza, the taste may even resemble that of a pizza, but it is not the real thing.

The Christian faith and pizza have more in common than you might think. With both, it is perfectly possible to settle for a pale imitation of the real thing. It may look bona fide; it may even have many of the same ingredients - but ultimately it is not authentic. And the trouble with a copy or counterfeit is that people make their minds up about something without ever having tried the real thing.

I guess what I am talking about here with regards to faith is a kind of spiritual mediocrity. It is second (or third) best and it puts people off Christianity forever. Truly going deep with God requires what Eugene Peterson calls 'A long obedience in the same direction'.[82] There is no quick fix - it is often slow and steady - it takes years, a lifetime in fact. It requires effort, determination and discipline. Although a living relationship with Jesus Christ is the free gift of God, such a relationship still requires an investment on our part. So many of us look for instant gratification today. Having to wait for something or worse still, work at it, is somewhat of an anathema. Not for the first time in history, we find that Christian faith is really rather counter-cultural!

When we work at it; when we employ disciplines and practices that shape our lives and orientate them towards God, then something special and lasting is formed deep within us; a kind of spiritual resilience is created that will stand the test of time. Think of it like a solid stake driven into the ground and then tied to a small sapling planted and growing and yet at the same time fragile and

---

[82] *A Long Obedience In The Same Direction*, Eugene Peterson, published by IVP, 1980

vulnerable. As the spiritual disciplines do their work, a greater attentiveness to the things of God emerges - me and my perspectives are changed.

When I was a child, on Sunday evenings my Dad would go off to church and my brother, sister and I would gather round a small electric organ with our mother who would play and sing old hymns from her upbringing. Oh the truth that is contained in some of those hymns! Here is one that comes to mind that perfectly sums up the point I am trying to make:

> Turn your eyes upon Jesus,
> Look full in His wonderful face,
> And the things of earth will grow strangely dim,
> In the light of His glory and grace.[83]

I am convinced that I am not the only one who is so easily blown off course by the transient distractions of this world. I am not the only one who wants to grow as a follower of Christ and yet wonders if I am making any progress at all. I am not the only one who needs a little structure and purpose in my life to facilitate that growth and help me keep my eyes upon Jesus.

The approach of adopting a Rule of Life is yielding dividends for me and it has helped others in the group that met together for 18 months as well. I commend both the concept and the content to you. I do however

---

[83] Hymn: *O Soul are you weary and troubled* by Helen H. Lemmel. Public Domain

recognise there is limited benefit in simply adopting my Rule. In part, I have shared my principles with you in the hope that they will stimulate your thinking. What are you passionate about? What has God put in your heart that just will not go away? What practices draw you closer to God? There will be some aspects of my Rule that you will want to include in yours and others that will not be for you. Other principles will come to your mind that you know you simply have to include.

So now it is over to you; it is time to draw up your Rule of Life. Please remember that while it can be aspirational, it must be achievable and realistic. If it is not, it will demotivate you rather than inspire you. Ultimately your Rule must serve as a purposeful tool to help you grow in your relationship with God.

As you begin this process, I offer you three steps to help you along the way:[84]

STEP 1: Be Reflective

Take time to reflect on your own spiritual journey to date. Are you growing? Whose responsibility is that? What direction do you want to move in? Where do you want to be in twelve months or two years' time?

STEP 2: Be Honest

What are the areas of weakness you would like to

---

[84] Steps by Stephen A. Macchia in his book, *Crafting A Rule Of Life*, published by IVP, 2012

personally address? What are the strengths you would like to develop still further? Remember it is important to be honest - resist the temptation to include principles you feel you ought to.

STEP 3: Be Specific

Which practices have proved helpful to you in the past? What habits or disciplines might be life-giving going forward?

1. ....

2. ....

3. ....

4. ....

5. ....

6. ....

7. ....

8. ....

9. ....

10. ....

11. ....

12. ....

I entitled this book 'For the Journey' because that is what all of us are on. We all know what it is like to get lost or take a wrong turn. We have all at one time or another embarked on a trip and ended up taking a very circuitous route to reach our destination. My prayer is that the content of this book and the thought processes in it have inspired you and will help you to journey well with God and to the destination He has planned. Enjoy the journey....

Further Reading

Baab, Lynne M, *Sabbath Keeping*, IVP, 2005

Belcher, Jim, *Deep Church*, IVP, 2009

Chester, Tim, *The Busy Christian's Guide To Busyness*, IVP, 2006

Costa, Ken, *God At Work*, Continuum, 2007

Draper, Brian, *Less Is More: Spirituality For Busy Lives*, Lion Hudson, 2012

Edwards, Joel, *An Agenda For Change*, Zondervan, 2008

Furtick, Steven, *Crash The Chatterbox*, Multnomah Books, 2014

Gempf, Conrad, *Mealtime Habits Of The Messiah*, Zondervan, 2005

Greene, Mark, *Thank God It's Monday*, Scripture Union Publishing, 2003

Hybels, Bill, *Simplify: Ten Practices To Unclutter Your Soul*, Hodder & Stoughton, 2015

Kruse, Kevin, *15 Secrets Successful People Know About Time Management*, The Kruse Group, 2015

Macchia, Stephen A, *Crafting A Rule Of Life*, IVP, 2012

Muller, Wayne, *Sabbath*, Bantam Books, 1999

Ortberg, John, *The Me I Want To Be*, Zondervan, 2010

Peterson, Eugene, *A Long Obedience In The Same Direction*, IVP, 1980

Scazzero, Peter, *Emotionally Healthy Spirituality*, Thomas Nelson, 2006

Warren, Rick, *The Daniel Plan*, Zondervan, 2013

Wright, Tom, *The Meal Jesus Gave Us*, SPCK, 1999

Printed in Great Britain
by Amazon

29427396R00084